Letter to the Sovereign, HM (1926 - 2022).

"An odd thought struck me; we shall receive no letters in the grave." Dr Samuel Johnson

TABLE OF CONTENTS:

PREFACE: Dr Ngozi Ekweremadu, a Nigerian whistleblower.

"Freedom of Expression is the cornerstone of our democracy." The Right Honourable Jacob Rees-Mogg (MP).

'Judiciary in England and Wales 'institutionally racist', says https://www.theguardian.com › law › oct › judiciary-[i...18 Oct 2022 — Exclusive: more than half of legal professionals in survey said they saw a judge acting in a racially biased way.'

"Gabon's Ali Bongo Ondimba Calls 'on the World to Make Noise." News

Uncle Tom: "Shit hole Africa." President Donald Trump.

"Freedom of Expression is a basic right." Lady Hale

BEDFORD, ENGLAND: District Judge Paul Robert Ayers, >70, a Mason, and the Senior Vice President of the Association of Her Majesty's District Judges of 3, St Paul's Square, MK 40 1SQ, you are drowning in debt. White man, let me tell you, the white ancestors of your own white mother and father were THIEVES and owners of stolen poor black children of defenceless AFRICANS, including the black African ancestors of Meghan Markle and her white children, and you are relatively very rich ONLY because African descendants of the robbed do not, yet, have overwhelming leverage necessary to demand and extract equitable reparation, and enforce the settlement of several centuries of unpaid accruing interest - Habakkuk.

Deluded fantasists: "Caribbean nations will demand $33 trillion (£26.5 trillion) and a formal apology from European countries over their role in the transatlantic slave trade." News

Only stupid Africans expect others to voluntarily relinquish several centuries-old advantageous positions – without overwhelming leverage, and only stupider Africans expect demons to cast out demons – Matthew 12:27.

Saxe-Coburg and Gotha families crossed the English Channels.

BEDFORD, ENGLAND: District Judge Paul Robert Ayers, >70, a Mason, and the Senior Vice President of the Association of Her Majesty's District Judges of 3, St Paul's Square, MK 40 1SQ, what's the real name of your own white father, where did he come from, and when? Or did white ancestors of your own white mother and father evolve from black monkeys with tails to tailless white monkeys in the forests of Freemasons' Kempston?

"Various theories have tried to prove that the Negro is a stage in the slow evolution of monkeys into man." Dr Frantz Fanon (1925 – 1961).

"We are just an advanced breed of monkeys on a minor planet of a very average star. But we can understand the Universe. That makes us something very special." — Dr Stephen Hawking (1942 – 2018).

The real name of Ghislaine Maxwell's dad was Ján Ludvík Hyman Binyamin Hoch (1923 – 1991), and he was a Jewish crook, and he came from Czechoslovakia in the 1940s. The crooked Jew lied all the time.

"Lies are told all time." Sir Michael Havers (1923 – 1992).

Latent, but very, very, potent Turf War: Closeted hereditary racist descendants of undocumented refugees from Eastern Europe, genetic aliens with arbitrarily acquired camouflage English names - whose ancestors crossed the English Channels, not that long ago, without luggage or decent shoes – oppress African descendants of the robbed with yields of the robbery - Habakkuk.

Before Slavery, what?

Based on available evidence, gigantic yields of SLAVERY, not feudal agriculture, lured Jews, including the ancestors of Benjamin Disraeli (1804 – 1881) to Great Britain.

Then, there was only subsistence feudal agriculture: "Agriculture not only gives riches to a nation, but the only one she can call her own." Dr Samuel Johnson

Very, very, charitable Freemasons: Half-educated school dropouts and their superiors who have informal access to some very, very, powerful white Freemason Judges – Habakkuk 1:4.

Facts are Holy, and Holiness cannot be overemphasised.

"They may not have been well written from a grammatical point of view but I am confident I had not forgotten any of the facts." Geraint Evans, NHS Postgraduate Tutor, Oxford, of Rowtree Dental Care, Rowtree Road, Northampton NN4 0NY.

Our scatter-head crooked white Welsh imbecile of our Empire of Stolen Affluence. Our closeted hereditary racist white Welsh imbecile Postgraduate Tutor, Oxford.

Based on several decades of very, very, proximate observations and direct experiences, their skin colour is universally acknowledged to be irrefutably superior, but their intellects aren't, and their legal system is fundamentally designed to conceal that truth – Habakkuk 1:4.

Northampton, England: GDC, Geraint Evans, NHS Postgraduate Tutor, Oxford, unrelentingly lied under implied oath (on record) – Habakkuk 1:4.

Our incompetently dishonest closeted hereditary racist white Welsh imbecile of our own Empire of Stolen Affluence – Habakkuk.

Had he been black, or had the Judges been black, he would have been in trouble.

Our imbecile crooked postgraduate tutor of our Empire of Stolen Affluence - Habakkuk.

Quasi-Communism: Bedford's District Judge Paul Robert Ayers, >70, a Mason, and the Senior Vice President of the Association of Her Majesty's District Judges of 3, St Paul's Square, MK 40 1SQ: Apart from creating very, very, cushy salaried jobs white Solicitors and Barristers (predominantly but not exclusively white), who FAILED in practise, and loads did, what do white imbeciles (predominantly but not exclusively white adults with the basic skills of a child) need very, very, expensive administration of English Law for?

Their bastardised, indiscreetly dishonest, unashamedly mediocre, vindictive, potently weaponised, and institutional RACIST legal system that was overseen by members of the Antichrist Freemasonry Quasi-Religion (Mediocre Mafia, New Pharisees, New Good Samaritans, Defenders of Faiths, including all exotic faiths and religions associated with the 15 Holy Books in the House of Commons, and Dissenters of the Faith – John 14:6) – Habakkuk 1:4.

"All sections of UK society are institutionally racist." Sir Bernard Hogan-Howe, KBE.

The Judiciary is part of UK society.

"The best opportunity of developing academically and emotional." Bedford's District Judge Paul Robert Ayers, >70, a Mason, and the Senior Vice President of the Association of Her Majesty's District Judges of 3, St Paul's Square, MK 40 1SQ, approved Judgement.

If the white man, albeit England's Class Senior Judge, read his approved Judgement, he was a FOOL, and if he didn't, he lied as he implied that he did. Based on cogent, irrefutable, and available evidence, the white ancestors of his white mother and father were incompetent racist LIARS too, they were THIEVES and owners of stolen poor black children of defenceless poor Africans, including the black African ancestors of Meghan Markle and her white children – Habakkuk.

Our incontrovertibly functional semi-illiterate Senior Judge of our Empire of Stolen Affluence. Poly-educated functional semi-illiterate closeted hereditary white supremacist plebeian approved and immortalised what white mother and father spoke, which his poly-educated white superiors and supervisors in LUTON authorised.

HHJ Perusko studied law at Poly: Not Russell Group Inferior Education – Proverbs 17:16.

Based on cogent, irrefutable, and available evidence, Bedford's District Judge Paul Robert Ayers, >70, a Mason, and the Senior Vice President of the Association of Her Majesty's District Judges of 3, St Paul's Square, MK 40 1SQ, unrelentingly lied under oath (approved Judgement) – Habakkuk 1:4. Google: The White Judge Lied.

Had he been black or had his white superiors and supervisors in LUTON been black, he would have been in trouble.

Negress, former Judge, Constance Briscoe (ugly), attempted to mislead the Police, she was punished.

"Michael Jackson would have been found guilty if he'd been black." Jo Brand

Our own Nigerien and Nigerian babies with huge uranium mines, and/or gigantic oil wells and gas fields near their huts eat only 1.5/day in our own shit hole AFRICA, very, very, bellyful, overfed, and overweight scatter-head, closeted hereditary racist white bastards (predominantly but not exclusively white) whose mothers and fathers have never seen crude oil, and whose children might not be able to spell uranium (OECD), and whose ancestors, including the white ancestors of unapologetic white supremacist Sir Winston Churchill (1874 – 1965), were fed like battery hens with yields of stolen poor black children of defenceless Africans, including the black African ancestors of Meghan Markle and her white children, thrive in Great Britain; which part of our shit hole AFRICA is great?

Then, everyone in Great Britain was white, including THIEVES, and gigantic yields of stolen children of defenceless Africans, including the black African ancestors of Meghan Markle and her white children, were used to build magnificent courts and pay the salaries of white Judges who sent white people who stole money to great prisons built with yields of stolen lives – Habakkuk.

Then, all Judges were white, and most of them were MASONS, and some of them were thicker than a gross of planks, and they lied to their own mentally gentler children and the white imbeciles who sat before them, (predominantly but not exclusively white adults with the basic of child) – that they were geniuses, and they destroyed all self-educated Negurs from shit hole AFRICA – who knew that they were closeted hereditary white supremacist bastards who sat on bones of stolen children of defenceless poor people, including the black African ancestors of Meghan Markle and her white children, and more bones than the millions of skulls at the doorstep of Comrade Pol Pot (1925 – 1998), in Grand Cathedral Courts preceded by SLAVERY, future flats. 29, Goldington Road is a block of flats.

A closeted hereditary racist white bastard saw two holes, Religious Psychosis and Hypothyroidism Psychosis, and he is trying to use them to destroy futures of African children, just as the white ancestors of his white mother and father,

and those they armed, used guns to rain hell fire on
Africans and their children – during several continuous
centuries of merciless racist evil. A racist descendant of
THIEVES and owners of stolen black children of
defenceless poor Africans, including the black African
ancestors of Meghan Markle and her white children. Then
in our tribe in the African bush, the closeted hereditary
racist white bastard would be treated with sticks and
stones.

"Stoning certainly teaches people a lesson." Ayatollah
Sadegh Khalkhali (1926 – 2003), Chief Justice, Supreme
Court, Iran

"The white man is the devil." Elijah Mohammed (1897 –
1975).

Based on several decades of very, very, proximate
observations and direct experiences, the white man is not
only the devil, but he is also a THIEF - Habakkuk.

BEDFORD, ENGLAND: GDC, Freemason, Brother
Richard Hill fabricated reports and unrelentingly lied under
oath – Habakkuk 1:4.

A very, very, dishonest closeted hereditary racist
Freemason of our Empire of Stolen Affluence - Habakkuk.

Had he been black, or had the Judges been black, he would
have been in trouble.

Bedford's District Judge Paul Robert Ayers, >70, a Mason, and the Senior Vice President of the Association of Her Majesty's District Judges of 3, St Paul's Square, MK 40 1SQ: What exactly are the purpose of Statutory Provisions, Civil Procedure Rules, and Precedent - in legal systems where white people, and only white people are allowed to fabricate reports and tell incompetent racist lies under oath – Habakkuk 1:4?

Based on several decades of very, very, proximate observations and direct experiences, their law is transparently equal for blacks and whites, but its administration is not, and the administration of any law is 'meat', and theirs is tyrant closeted hereditary white supremacist Freemasons' tool – Habakkuk 1:4.

"Rightful liberty is unobstructed action according to our will within limits drawn around us by the equal rights of others. I do not add 'within the limits of the law' because law is often but the tyrant's will, and always so when it violates the rights of the individual." President Thomas Jefferson (1743 – 1826).

Bedford's District Judge Paul Robert Ayers, >70, a Mason, and the Senior Vice President of the Association of Her Majesty's District Judges of 3, St Paul's Square, MK 40 1SQ: He sat on a very, very, highchair that the people of Bedford couldn't and didn't buy, in our cathedral court that was preceded by SLAVERY - Habakkuk.

Ignorant closeted hereditary racist bastards see molecules and they destroy all self-educated Africans who see atoms.

Our own Messiah saw quarks, but Jews, Romans, and others, saw molecules, and since they had brainlessly self-awarded the supreme knowledge, He was lynched like Gadhafi and crucified only because He spoke. The fellow was not punished for disclosing pictures His infinite mind painted, He was jumped on by very, very, very, shallow intolerant lunatic bastards – solely to prevent the only transparent Judge (John 5:22, Matthew 25:31-46), from speaking.

C of E raises serious concerns about Christian Freemasons
https://www.theguardian.com › uk-news › feb › c-of-e-…
8 Feb 2018 - Church of England warning that secret society may not be compatible with Christianity echoes concerns from 1987.

Then, all Judges were white, and most of them were Masons, and some of them were thicker than a gross of planks. Then, all semi-illiterate white Judges were RACIST FREEMASONS.

Your Majesty, in Heaven, nearer our Father in Heaven, closeted hereditary white supremacist demigods who brainlessly and baselessly self-awarded supreme knowledge, and wear very, very, very, vulgar Pharisees' charitable works as cloaks of deceit, and use very, very, very, expensive colourful and shiny aprons, with tacky ostentatious embroideries - to decorate the temples of their powerless and useless fertility tools, and lie that they don't lie, but tell incompetent racist lies, and all the time – Psalm 144, are very, very, very, powerful Voodoo Men, and they are demigods, but they are not our God, as only Christ is Lord, and our own Messiah is the only transparent Judge, and He will Judge all crooked Freemason Judges with the divine sword of transparent truth, and not Jonathan Aitken's deceptive sword of truth. Proverbs 15:3, John 5:22. Matthew 25:31-46.

Baba mi ni oko ayokele, osi tun lesin. Baba ni owo, osi ni oogun. Ifura ni oogun awon agbalagba, ifura paapa, alagbalagba oogun ni. Ewu nbe loko Alonge. Alonge paapa, ewu ni.

https://www.youtube.com/watch?v=BlpH4hG7m1A

Your Majesty, in Heaven, near our Father in Heaven, whenever it becomes a basic right for all, including self-educated sh*t hole Africans, such as your former obedient servant and subject, to disclose any truth, including politically incorrect truths, supported by hard evidence, Antichrist closeted white supremacist Freemasonry Quasi-Religion (Mediocre Mafia, New Pharisees, New Good Samaritans, Defenders of Faiths, including all religions and faiths associated with the 15 Holy Books in the House of Commons, and Dissenters of the Faith — John 14:6), will die, and instantly.

INTRODUCTION: Letter to the Sovereign, HM (1926 – 2022)

"There is not a truth existing which I fear or would wish unknown to the whole world." President Thomas Jefferson (1743 – 1826).

Then, Africans aided and abetted very, very, highly civilised, and ultra-righteous European Christians with the evil commerce of carrying and selling millions of stolen African children, including from Gabon (formerly unbounded and unmarked area of the West African bush), now, Africans aid and abet very, very, highly civilised, and super enlightened, but very greedy Europeans in stealing Africa's natural resources.

Your Majesty, in Heaven, near our Father in Heaven, if I may ask, what exactly is the point of Civil Procedure Rules (CPR), Statute, and Precedent if verdicts prior agreed, secretly, in Masons' Temples must be realised in open courts, and where it is dishonesty or perjury only if members of the Antichrist closeted white supremacist Freemasonry Quasi-Religion (Mediocre Mafia, New Pharisees, New Good Samaritans, Defenders of Faiths, including all religions and faiths associated with the 15 Holy Books in the House of Commons, and Dissenters of the Faith — John 14:6) — did not prior authorise it?

BEDFORD, ENGLAND: GDC, Freemason, Brother, Richard William Hill (Our NHS Postgraduate Tutor of our

Empire of Stolen Affluence) fabricated reports and unrelentingly lied under oath — Habakkuk 1:4.

Our very, very, dishonest white Stonemason.

Our Racist Crooked Mason NHS Postgraduate Tutor of our Empire of Stolen Affluence.

Our ultra-righteous racist white Freemason bastard: Their people are everywhere, and they control almost everything in Great Britain – Habakkuk 1:4.

Our ignorant descendant of very, very, highly civilised, super-enlightened, and devout Christian bastards and owners of stolen poor black children of defenceless Africans, including the black African ancestors of the white great grandchildren of Prince Phillip (1921–2021).

Philippians 1:21: Was Phillip a 33rd Degree Mason, Scottish Rite?

It is excessively stupid to suggest that being part of our indiscreetly institutionally racist system, where white people, and only white people, are allowed to fabricate reports and tell incompetent racist lies under oath is worth dying for — Habakkuk 1:4.

BEDFORD, ENGLAND: District Judge Paul Robert Ayers, >70, a Mason, and the Senior Vice President of the Association of Her Majesty's District Judges of 3, St Paul's Square, MK 40 1SQ, let me tell you, you are a historical imbecile, particularly economic history. Your ancestors were THIEVES and owners of stolen poor black children of defenceless Africans, including the black African ancestors of Meghan Markle and her white children – Habakkuk.

Based on cogent, irrefutable, and available evidence, properly rehearsed ultra-righteousness, and deceptively schooled civilised decorum were preceded by several continuous centuries of merciless racist evil: The greediest economic cannibalism and the evilest racist terrorism the world will ever know - Habakkuk.

Then, the white ancestors of your white mother and father were greedier than the grave, and like death, the armed racist white bastards — were never satisfied — Habakkuk 2:5.

Then, only one side had good guns and, expectedly, did all the killing. Google: Imagbon 1892.

Ultra-righteousness and deceptively schooled civilised decorum without equitable and transparently just reparation and the full settlement of several continuous centuries of unpaid accruing interest - are continuing RACIST FRAUD.

God Almighty did not create sh*t hole Africa, poor Africa, and Africans, based on cogent, irrefutable, and available evidence, insatiably greedy racist bastard European Christians invented poverty in Africa.

"How Europe underdeveloped Africa." Dr Walter Rodney (1942–1980).

The rumour in some pubs in Bedford, including Nag's Head — is that you are a Jew.

Rumour is not fact, and anyone who has tried to make fire in the African bush will confirm that there could be smoke without fire.

It is the absolute truth that gigantic yields of millions of stolen poor black children of defenceless Africans, including the African ancestors of Meghan Markle and her white children, not subsistence feudal agriculture, lured Jews, including the ancestors of Nigel Lawson and Benjamin Disraeli (1804–1881) — to Great Britain — Habakkuk.

WHITE PRIVILEGE: Let me tell you, you're worthy ONLY because of the universally acknowledged irrefutably superior skin colour that you neither made nor chose, and because England is relatively very, very, rich, apart from those, you are purified froth, ABSOLUTELY NOTHING.

"Affluence is not a birth right." David Cameron, a former Premier.

Just like our Universe, our Empire did not evolve from NOTHING, then, almost everything was actively and deliberately stolen with good guns — Habakkuk.

CHAPTER ONE: Dr Ngozi Ekweremadu, a Nigerian whistleblower

"**S**tudy history, study history, in history lies all the secrets of statecraft." Sir Winston Churchill (1874–1965).

OXFORD, ENGLAND: GDC, Bristol University Educated Mrs Helen Falcon, Member of the Most Excellent Order of our Empire (MBE), a former Member of the GDC Committee, a former Postgraduate Dean, Oxford, a very, very, charitable Rotarian (auxiliary Freemason), and the only spouse of Mr Falcon, unrelentingly lied under oath (on record)—Habakkuk 1:4.

Our very, very, dishonest white cougar. Our closeted hereditary racist Member of the Most of Excellent Order of our Empire of stolen affluence—Habakkuk.

Your Majesty in Heaven, near our Father in Heaven, the action of GDC, Bristol University Educated Mrs Helen Falcon, Member of the Most Excellent Order of our Empire (MBE), a former Member of the GDC Committee, a former Postgraduate Dean, Oxford, a very, very, charitable Rotarian (auxiliary Freemason), and the only spouse of Mr Falcon, is what RACIAL INTOLERANCE looks like from the perspective of Negurs.

Racial hatred is not a myth, and it is not extinct, and it is considerably more common than ordinarily realised, and before it unravels, it is a conspiracy theory, and when it does, it instantly mutates to a mistake.

"White supremacy is real, and it needs to be shattered." Dr Cornel West

Based on cogent, irrefutable, and available evidence, the entire foundation of Bristol City, including Bristol University where Mrs Helen Falcon, MBE, studied tooth science, one of the least academic branch of the sciences, before becoming a mere dmf (Community Dentist), one of the least academic specialities of one the least academic branch of the sciences, was built on bones of stolen poor black children of defenceless Africans, including the African ancestors of Meghan Markle and her white children, more bones than the millions of skulls at the doorstep of Comrade Pol Pot (1925–1998)—Habakkuk.

"An odd thought struck me; we shall receive no letters in the grave." Dr Samuel Johnson (1709 – 1784).

Your Majesty in Heaven, near our Father in Heaven, Dr Samuel Johnson did not receive letters in his grave, at the Westminster Abbey, because he couldn't, as he has no valid address, but if, like you, he is in Heaven, he will read this open letter, which is accessible to Christ and all the those who reside in Jannah.

"Jesus is the bedrock of my faith." HM (1926 – 2022).

Your Majesty in Heaven, near our Father in Heaven, if reasoning and vision do not have finite boundaries, it is soundly deductible that the fellow is who He says He is, and He told the truth before Jews and Romans, in the Council,

when He disclosed pictures His unbounded mind painted –
John 14:6.

******

Address: Heaven.

To: Our Revered Sovereign, HM (1926 – 2022), the
Defender of our own Faith (John 14:6), and like James, a
devout and obedient Slave of our own Messiah – of blessed
memory.

Dearest HM (1926 – 2022), a humble, obedient, and devout
servant of Christ – of blessed memory,

Re: An open letter from your self-educated African former
subject and obedient servant.

Your Majesty in Heaven, near our Father in Heaven, why
was He the bedrock of your faith? My hairs stood on end
when the defender of our own faith openly declared her
unalloyed belief in the exceptionalism of the fellow, and
before the whole world - John 14:6.

"Bi mo ba ronu ni pa Edumare, ara mi asi gbonriri bi oye ti
nse omo tuntun, ohun ti ofe fi nise ni emi ko mo, a mo osa
deru ba mi saa." Olarenwaju Adepoju.

He was lynched like Gadhafi and crucified only because He spoke; He disclosed pictures His unbounded mind painted.

Was He lynched like Gadhafi and crucified because He lied, or was he savagely beaten up because He was a lunatic?

Your Majesty in Heaven, near our Father in Heaven, bodily suffering is an evil, an evil Ne Plus Ultra.

Your Majesty in Heaven, near our Father in Heaven, the fellow was lynched like Gadhafi and crucified, by intolerant Jews and Romans, solely to prevent Him from speaking.

"Freedom of Expression is a basic right." Lady Hale: Freedom of Expression was part of the last Queen's Speech.

Matthew 14: John was jailed only because he spoke, and an intolerant lunatic Jew, King Herod, removed his head solely to prevent him from speaking.

Your Majesty in Heaven, near our Father in Heaven, based on cogent, irrefutable, and available evidence, due process, statute, civil procedure rules, and precedent under bendable, breakable, and indiscreetly institutionally racist administration of English law are properly rehearsed Charitable Antichrist Freemasons' scams – Habakkuk 1:4.

Your Majesty in Heaven, near our Father in Heaven: Based on very, very, proximate observations, direct experiences, and available evidence, the administration of English law is an irreparable, closeted hereditary white supremacists, Charitable, Antichrist Freemasons' scam – Habakkuk 1:4.

Our own Nigeria: Shell's docile cash cow since 1956: Unlike Putin's Russia, there are no oil wells or gas fields in LUTON and where the white mother and father of Bedford's District Judge Paul Robert Ayers, >70, a Mason, and the Senior Vice President of the Association of Her Majesty's District Judges of 3, St Paul's Square, MK 40 1SQ, were born.

Facts are sacred.

The truth allows no choice." Dr Samuel Johnson (1709 – 1784).

Our own Nigerian babies with huge oil wells and gas fields near their huts eat only 1.5/day in our own Nigeria, our bellyful, verifiably functional semi-illiterate, and closeted hereditary white supremacist bastard whose white mother and father have never seen crude oil, and whose white ancestors, including ultra-righteous John Bunyan (1628 – 1688), were fed like battery hens with yields of stolen poor black children of defenceless Africans, including the African ancestors of Meghan Markle and her white children, was our

Senior District Judge in Bedford, Great Britain, what's great about unashamed mediocrity?

Google: Mediocre Great England.

"Many Scots masters were considered among the most brutal, with life expectancy on their plantations averaging a mere four years. We worked them to death then simply imported more to keep the sugar and thus the money flowing. Unlike centuries of grief and murder, an apology cost nothing. So, what does Scotland have to say?" Herald Scotland: Ian Bell, Columnist, Sunday 28 April 2013

Our ultra-righteous hereditary racist white bastard. Our ignorant descendant of THIEVES and owners of stolen lives – Habakkuk.

Creeping DPRK.

BEDFORD, ENGLAND: District Judge Paul Robert Ayers, >70, a Mason, and the Senior Vice President of the Association of Her Majesty's District Judges of 3, St Paul's Square, MK 40 1SQ, based on cogent, irrefutable, and available evidence, you are incontrovertibly a functional semi-illiterate, unlike Putin's Russia, there are no oil wells or gas fields in LUTON and where your own white mother and father were born, you are a very, very, patriotic white Briton, you are relatively rich, and you dishonestly implied that you did not know that the white ancestors of your own white mother and father were THIEVES and owners of stolen poor black children of defenceless Africans, including the black African ancestors of Meghan Markle and her white children – Habakkuk.

Wilful ignorance is deceptive and malicious.

OYINBO OMO OLE. OYINBO OMO ALE.

"The supreme vice is shallowness." Wilde

BEDFORD, ENGLAND: District Judge Paul Robert Ayers, >70, a Mason, and the Senior Vice President of the Association of Her Majesty's District Judges of 3, St Paul's Square, MK 40 1SQ: If your white mother and father did not tell you that equitable reparation pends, and several centuries of unpaid interest accrue, they wilfully lied to you (dishonest), or they were recklessly ignorant.

Recklessness is malice.

"I do not approve of anything that tampers with natural ignorance. Ignorance is like a delicate exotic fruit; touch it and the bloom is gone. The whole theory of modern education is radically unsound. Fortunately, in England, at any rate, education produces no effect whatsoever. If it did, it would prove a serious danger to the upper classes, and probably lead to acts of violence in Grosvenor Square." Wilde

Ignorance is bliss.

CHAPTER TWO: Letter to the Sovereign, HM (1926 – 2022).

"Those who know the least obey the best." George Farquhar (1677–1707).

BEDFORD, ENGLAND: District Judge Paul Robert Ayers, >70, a Mason, and the Senior Vice President of the Association of Her Majesty's District Judges of 3, St Paul's Square, MK 40 1SQ: Our functional semi-illiterate, vindictive, and hereditary racist hyper patriotic white man, let me tell you, you're rich ONLY because African descendants of the robbed do not, yet, have overwhelming power (leverage) necessary to demand and extract equitable and just REPARATION, and enforce the settlement of several centuries of unpaid accruing interest – Habakuk.

Based on available evidence, our own money, NIGERIA (oil/gas), is by far more relevant to the economic survival of all your own white children, your white spouse, your white mother, and your white father than Freemasons' Kempston. Unlike Putin's Russia, there are no oil wells or gas fields in LUTON, and where your own white mother and father were born. The white ancestors of your own white father and mother were THIEVES and owners of stolen poor black children of defenceless poor people, including the black African ancestors of Meghan Markle and her white children - Habakkuk.

Our hyper patriotic genetic alien with arbitrarily acquired camouflage English names. The only evidence of the purportedly very, very, very, very, High IQ of the poly-educated functional semi-illiterate plebeian, a direct descendant of peasants (mere agricultural labourers) from Eastern Europe, who crossed the English Channels, not that long ago, without luggage or decent shoes, is the stolen affluence that his thoroughly wretched ancestors crossed the English Channels to latch onto—Habakkuk.

Before Slavery, what?

Then, there was only subsistence feudal agriculture.

"Agriculture not only gives riches to a nation, but the only one she can call her own." Dr Samuel Johnson

Hyper-patriotism: The secure mask of assimilating genetic aliens.

"Patriotism is the last refuge of a scoundrel." Dr Samuel Johnson.

If, in the bush of sh*t hole West Africa, a Negur farmed loads of white pigs, with great pink snouts, for meat, the stupidest of the white pigs, with great pink snouts, deserves to be the first to be killed and eaten.

"There is no sin except stupidity." Wilde

"I am very fond of my pigs, but that doesn't stop me from eating them." Archbishop Runcie (1921–2000).

"All sections of UK society are institutionally racist." Sir Bernard Hogan-Howe, a former Metropolitan Police Chief.

The English Judiciary is part of UK society.

"The best opportunity of developing academically and emotional." Bedford's District Judge Paul Robert Ayers, >70, a Mason, and the Senior Vice President of the Association of Her Majesty's District Judges of 3, St Paul's Square, MK 40 1SQ.

Brainless nonsense: Our closeted hereditary racist white dunce of our Empire of Stiken Affluence.

Facts are sacred.

"The truth allows no choice." Dr Samuel Johnson

OYINBO OMO OLE: OYINBO OMO ALE.

"Yes, Sir, it does her honour, but it would do nobody else honour. I have indeed not read it all. But when I take up the end of a web, and find a packthread, I do not expect, by looking further, to find embroidery." Dr Samuel Johnson.

Our brainless racist white bastard employed the World's language like a prostitute from our own oil and gas rich Nigeria — who is in Great Britain to study symmetrical eyebrows decoration.

BEDFORD, ENGLAND: District Judge Paul Robert Ayers, >70, a Mason, and the Senior Vice President of the Association of Her Majesty's District Judges of 3, St Paul's

Square, MK 40 1SQ, our poly-educated racist white rubbish approved and immortalised what his semi-illiterate white mother and father spoke, which his poly-educated white supervisors in LUTON authorised.

HHJ Perusko studied Law at Poly: Not Russell Group Inferior Education — Proverbs 17:16.

Perception is grander than reality.

Based on several decades of very, very, proximate observations and direct experiences, the white man is grossly overrated.

"Find the truth and tell it—Harold Pinter (1930–2008).

https://www.youtube.com/watch?v=BlpH4hG7m1A

"I know of no evil that has ever existed, nor can imagine any evil to exist, worse than the tearing of eighty thousand persons annually from their native land, by a combination of the most civilised nations inhabiting the most enlightened part of the globe, but more especially under the sanction of the laws of that Nation which calls herself the most free and the most happy of them all." Prime Minister William Pitt the Younger

Very, very, greedy hereditary racist white bastards who shipped millions of bad guns to Africa – in exchange for more millions of stolen poor black children of defenceless Africans, including the African ancestors of Meghan

Markle and her white children – were very, very, very, bellyful, free, and happy, but those who shipped millions of guns to Africa, among those who did not evolve to treat penetrative gunshot wounds, were neither civilised nor enlightened - Habakkuk.

Based on cogent, irrefutable, and available evidence, then, about 200,000 made in Birmingham guns were shipped to Africa – annually, in exchange for kidnapped poor black African children, including the black African ancestors of Meghan Markle and her white children - Habakkuk

"It was our arms in the river of Cameroon, put into the hands of the trader, that furnished him with the means of pushing his trade; and I have no more doubt that they are British arms, put into the hands of Africans, which promote universal war and desolation that I can doubt their having done so in that individual instance. I have shown how great is the enormity of this evil, even on the supposition that we take only convicts and prisoners of war. But take the subject in another way, and how does it stand? Think of 80,000 persons carried out of their native country by, we know not what means! For crimes imputed! For light or inconsiderable faults! For debts perhaps! For the crime of witchcraft! Or a thousand other weak or scandalous pretexts! Reflect on 80,000 persons annually taken off! There is something in the horror of it that surpasses all bounds of imagination." – Prime Minister William Pitt the Younger

Bedford's District Judge Paul Robert Ayers, >70, a Mason, and the Senior Vice President of the Association of Her Majesty's District Judges of 3, St Paul's Square, MK 40 1SQ, white man, let me tell you, properly rehearsed ultra-righteousness and deceptively schooled civilised decorum were preceded by several continuous centuries of merciless RACIST EVIL: The greediest economic cannibalism and the evilest racist terrorism the world will ever know – Habakkuk.

"England is like a prostitute who, having sold her body all her life, decides to quit her business, and then tells everybody that she wants to be chaste and protect her flesh as if it were jade." He Manzi

Then, everyone in Great Britain was white, very, very, highly civilised, and super-enlightened, and there were European civilisation and laws — based on Christian belief, and yields of millions of stolen poor black children of defenceless Africans, including the African ancestors of Meghan Markle and her white children, were used to build magnificent Cathedral Courts, such as Bedford County Court, 3, St Paul's Square, MK40 1SQ, and pay the Salaries of white Judges who sent white people who stole money to Grand Prisons built with yields of stolen and destroyed black lives — Habakkuk.

Sir, Mr Justice Haddon-Cave, KC, KBE, based on cogent, irrefutable, and available evidence, the Grand Royal Courts

of Justice, Strand — were preceded by Slavery; it paid for
them— Habakkuk.

CHAPTER THREE: Dr Ngozi Ekweremadu, a Nigerian whistleblower

"**M**r Bamgbelu clearly has very, very strong views about education and I understand those views are based upon the fact that he is a successful dentist here in Bedford which he attributes to the fact that his parents cared for him and his education when he was young. They ensured that he had a proper fee paying education…….." Bedford's District Judge Paul Robert Ayers, >70, a Mason, and the Senior Vice President of the Association of Her Majesty's District Judges of 3, St Paul's Square, MK 40 1SQ – proofed and approved Judgement.

PURIFIED ROT!

West Africans should be able to detect when closeted hereditary white supremacist Freemason Judges are talking ROT.

Based on available evidence, Meghan Markle is 43% West African.

"Gentlemen, you are now about to embark on a course of studies which will occupy you for two years. Together, they form a noble adventure. But I would like to remind you of an important point. Nothing that you will learn in the course of your studies will be of the slightest possible use to you in after life, save only this, that if you work hard and intelligently you should be able to detect when a man is talking rot, and that, in my view, is the main, if not the sole, purpose of education." John Alexander Smith, Philosopher (1863 – 1939)

Bedford's District Judge Paul Robert Ayers, >70, a Mason, and the Senior Vice President of the Association of Her Majesty's District Judges of 3, St Paul's Square, MK 40 1SQ: His universally acknowledged irrefutably superior skin colour - that he neither made nor chose - concealed a dark his black brain.

Financial disclosure in a divorce: 'How can a Negur, a mere Nigerian, have what I do not have?'

OYINBO OMO OLE: OYINBO OMO ALE.

Then, when siblings, hereditary racial hatred, and uncontrollable indiscreet envy, engage in sensuous incestuous coitus, loads of it, insanity was their offspring.

"To disagree with three—fourths of the British public on all points is one of the first elements of sanity, one of the deepest consolations in all moments of spiritual doubt." Wilde.

An incontrovertibly functional semi-illiterate closeted hereditary racist white bastard: Universally acknowledged irrefutably superior skin colour, stolen trust fund, and what else?

Based on observations and direct experiences, all functional semi-illiterate white Freemason Judges are RACISTS.

Very, very, poor in natural resources. Unlike Putin's Russia, there are no oil wells or gas fields in Freemasons' Kempston and where his own white mother and father were born. Several continuous centuries of stealing and slavery preceded the huge stolen trust fund – Habakkuk.

WHITE PRIVILEGE: Only his universally acknowledged irrefutably superior skin colour and God Almighty are truly good (Mark 10:18), and he neither made nor chose it, and he will be considerably diminished as a human being without the invaluable visible morphology, and he knows it.

Indiscreet envy: "Envy is weak." Yul Brynner.

Brainless, poly-educated class, sarcasm: Envy is a thief.

It is plainly deductible that the white father and mother of Bedford's District Judge Paul Robert Ayers, >70, a Mason, and the Senior Vice President of the Association of Her Majesty's District Judges of 3, St Paul's Square, MK 40

1SQ, did not have very, very strong views about education, and they did not care, had they, their functional semi-illiterate white son would not have studied law at Poly, and he would not approved and immortalised excessive stupidity at 16, and he would be a properly educated lawyer, privately educated Anthony Julius, Anthony Blair, Geoff Hoon, and Rabinder Singh's - Class, and he might practice proper law in STRAND, instead of daily dialogues with white imbeciles in BEDFORD (predominantly but not exclusively white adults with the basic skills of a child) – Habakkuk 1:4.

Your Majesty in Heaven, near our Father in Heaven, based on observations and direct experiences, all white Freemason Judges (predominantly but not exclusively white) who expended their professional lives on daily dialogues with white imbeciles (predominantly but not exclusively white adults with the basic skills of a child), were, expectedly, affected by their regular encounters, they became very, very, very, very, dull.

"Sir, he was dull in company, dull in his closet, dull everywhere. He was dull in a new way, and that made many people think him GREAT…." Dr Samuel Johnson

Why should the white mother and father of Bedford's District Judge Paul Robert Ayers, >70, a Mason, and the Senior Vice President of the Association of Her Majesty's District Judges of 3, St Paul's Square, MK 40 1SQ, need very, very, very, strong views about education when there is cogent and irrefutable evidence that the white ancestors of his white mother and father, including the white ancestors of white, and unapologetic white supremacist, Winston Churchill (1874 – 1965), were THIEVES: Extremely nasty, vicious, and merciless racist murderers, industrial-scale professional armed robbers, armed land grabbers, gun runners, drug dealers (opium merchants), and owners of millions of stolen poor black children of defenceless Africans, including the West African ancestors of Meghan Markle and her white children – Habakkuk?

BEDFORD, ENGLAND: District Judge Paul Robert Ayers, >70, a Mason, and the Senior Vice President of the Association of Her Majesty's District Judges of 3, St Paul's Square, MK 40 1SQ, money is meat. It is not the yield of your land or your talent. Your white ancestors were THIEVES and owners of stolen poor children of defenceless AFRICANS, including the black African ancestors of Meghan Markle and her white children. Then, almost everything was actively and deliberately stolen with GUNS - Habakkuk.

CONFLICT OF INTEREST. New Herod, Matthew 2:16: They lied to their mentally gentler children and the white imbeciles (predominantly but not exclusively white adults with the basic skills of a child) – they shepherd - that they are geniuses, and they vindictively destroy all self-educated Africans who know that they are not.

Facts are Holy, and they cannot be overstated.

"I believe truth, the prime attribute of the Deity, and death an eternal sleep, at least of the body." Lord Byron (1788 – 1824).

CHAPTER FOUR. Letter to the Sovereign, HM (1926 - 2022).

"**Jesus** is the bedrock of my faith." HM (1926 – 2022).

Your Majesty in Heaven, near our Father in Heaven, if it cannot be disproved that reasoning and vision are infinite, it is soundly deductible that the fellow is who He says He is, and He told the truth before Jews and Romans, in the Council, when He disclosed pictures His unbounded mind painted – John 14:6.

Mustafa Mehmet is Turkish, but Boris Johnson isn't.

The real name of the patriarch of Boris Johnson was Ali Kamal, and the devout Muslim came from Turkey in the early 20th century.

BEDFORD, ENGLAND: District Judge **Paul Robert Ayers, >70, a Mason,** and the Senior Vice President of the Association of Her Majesty's District Judges of 3, St Paul's Square, MK 40 1SQ, what is the real name of your own white father, where did he come from, and when? Or did the white ancestors of your white father and mother evolve from black monkeys with tails to tailless white monkeys in LUTON, or the Epping Forest?

OYINBO ODE: Superior skin colour conceals a dark black brain.

Based on available evidence, Freemasonry Quasi-Religion is not Goldman Sachs, and those who nearly passed or just passed at school could join the Satanic Closeted White Supremacist Vulgarly Charitable Network.

Bedford's District Judge Paul Robert Ayers, >70, a Mason, and the Senior Vice President of the Association of Her Majesty's District Judges of 3, St Paul's Square, MK 40 1SQ: Our incontrovertibly functional semi-illiterate white man, albeit England's Class Senior District Judge, should use his brain for the benefit of his own white children. What will Mason Judges do if they didn't control the Police Force and the Judiciary? Then, in the dormitories, at Anglican Church Grammar School, their type must defend themselves with words or their fists.

BEDFORD, ENGLAND: GDC, Sue Gregory, Officer of the Most Excellent Order of our Empire, unrelentingly lied under implied oath (on record)—Habakkuk 1:4. A very, very, dishonest white woman. A racist crooked Officer of the Most Excellent Order of our Empire of Stolen Affluence—Habakkuk.

BEDFORD, ENGLAND: GDC, Freemason, Brother, Richard William Hill fabricated reports and unrelentingly lied under oath – Habakkuk 1:4.

A very, very, dishonest white man. A racist crooked Freemason.

Your Majesty in Heaven, near our Father in Heaven, then, and only there, it was a crime only if the true rulers of the state, the very, very, righteous, and selfless members of the very, very, charitable Antichrist Freemasonry Quasi-Religion (Mediocre Mafia, New Pharisees, New Good Samaritans, Defenders of Faiths, including all the faiths and religions associated with the 15 Holy Books in the House of Commons – Habakkuk 1:4, did not prior authorise the racist crime.

Habakkuk 1:4: Your Majesty in Heaven, near our Father in Heaven, then, and only there, everything was based on incompetent racist lies, and verdicts were prior agreed in the Temples of Antichrist Freemasons, Defenders of Faiths, and Dissenters of the Faith – John 14:6, and in the open court, incompetent art incompetently guards, guides, and imitates purportedly real life.

Your Majesty in Heaven, near our Father in Heaven, unlike you, racist white criminals (predominantly but not exclusively white privileged dullards), were not and, are not deterred by the transparent Justice of the only Judge that matters (John 5:22, Matthew 25: 31- 46), as they do not believe in His exceptionalism – John 14:6.

Under which Statute, or Sections, ad/or Subsections of English Law, or Precedent, or Civil Procedure Rules – did GDC, Sue Gregory, Officer of the Most Excellent Order of our Empire (OBE), unrelentingly tell incompetent racist lies under implied oath (on record) – Habakkuk 1:4.

Your Majesty in Heaven, near our Father in Heaven, English Law and its administration are inseparable chains, and if any part is bad, crooked, or institutionally racist, all is unsafe: Falsus in uno, falsus in omnibus.

Your Majesty in Heaven, near our Father in Heaven, English Law is equal for African Negroes and Caucasians, but its administration is not, and the administration of English Law is its meat.

Your Majesty in Heaven, near our Father in Heaven, not every aspect of the administration of English Law is tyrants' tool.

"Rightful liberty is unobstructed action according to our will within limits drawn around us by the equal rights of others. I do not add 'within the limits of the law' because law is often but the tyrant's will, and always so when it violates the rights of the individual." President Thomas Jefferson (1743 – 1826).

Bedford's District Judge Paul Robert Ayers, >70, a Mason, and the Senior Vice President of the Association of Her

Majesty's District Judges of 3, St Paul's Square, MK 40
1SQ: Poly-educated racist white rubbish was granted the
platform to display hereditary prejudice. He rides a very,
very, tiger, deluded, he thinks he's it, dismounted, he will
instantly revert to NOTHING. A mere former debt-collector
Solicitor in Norwich: A former 5th Rate Partner in Norwich.
Only his universally acknowledged irrefutably superior skin
colour and God Almighty are truly good — Mark 10:18, and
he neither made nor chose it, and he will be considerably
diminished as a human being without it, and he knows it.

Bedford's District Judge Paul Robert Ayers, >70, a Mason,
and the Senior Vice President of the Association of Her
Majesty's District Judges of 3, St Paul's Square, MK 40
1SQ: An ignorant racist white leech; a
righteous descendant of ultra-righteous WHITE
PROFESSIONAL THIEVES and owners of stolen children
of defenceless poor people, including the African ancestors
of Meghan Markle's white children - Habakkuk.

Which part of our Grand Cathedral, Bedford County Court,
3, St Paul's Square, MK40 1SQ, was not stolen, or which
part of it is the yield of the Higher IQ of your own white
mother and father, or which part of it did transparent virtue
yield, or which part of it did the very, very, good people of
Bedford buy, or which part of it preceded the barbarously
racist traffic in millions of stolen children of defenceless
poor people: The building or its chattels?

OYINBO OLE: WHITE THIEVES: HABAKKUK.

Ignorance is bliss.

"Those who know the least obey the best." George Farquhar

An ignorant racist white bastard. An ultra-righteous descendant of economic migrants with camouflage English names, and a very hardened racist leech. A righteous descendant of THIEVES and owners of stolen children of defenceless poor people, including the African ancestors of Meghan Markle's white children – Habakkuk.

"Affluence is not birth right." David Cameron, a former Premier.

Bedford's District Judge Paul Robert Ayers, >70, a Mason, and the Senior Vice President of the Association of Her Majesty's District Judges of 3, St Paul's Square, MK 40 1SQ: The only evidence of his purportedly Higher IQ is the stolen affluence that his thoroughly wretched ancestors, genetic aliens, crossed the English Channels, without luggage or decent shoes to latch onto, and they arbitrarily acquired camouflage English names, blended, and latched onto the gigantic yields of several continuous centuries of merciless racist evil: The greediest economic cannibalism and the evilest racist terrorism the world will ever know – Habakkuk.

BEDFORD, ENGLAND: Your Majesty, based on cogent, irrefutable, and available evidence, GDC, Sue Gregory,

Officer of the Most Excellent Order of our Empire (OBE), unrelentingly lied under implied oath (on record) – Habakkuk 1:4.

A very, very, dishonest white woman.

A very, very, crooked, closeted hereditary white supremacist Officer of the Most Excellent Order of our Empire of Stolen Affluence – Habakkuk.

Their bastardised, unashamedly mediocre, indiscreetly dishonest, vindictive, potently weaponised, and institutionally racist legal system that is overseen by members of the very, very, charitable Antichrist Freemasonry Quasi-Religion (Mediocre Mafia, New Pharisees, New Good Samaritans, Defenders of Faiths, including all the Faiths associated with the 15 Holy Books in the House of Commons, and Dissenters of the Faith – John 14:6).

Your Majesty, as you are now nearer the throne of the only transparently true Judge, in heaven, you will know that He is colour-blind, and transparently just – John 5:22, Matthew 25: 31 -46.

Your Majesty, it was plainly deductible that then, it would have been absolutely impossible for GDC, Sue Gregory, Officer of the Most Excellent Order of our Empire (OBE), to resort to unrelentingly incompetent mendacity, under implied oath (on record) – Habakkuk 1:4, without the prior approval of the true rulers of the state.

Your Majesty, GDC, Sue Gregory, Officer of the Most Excellent Order of our Empire (OBE), unrelentingly lied under implied oath (on record) – Habakkuk 1:4, and by so doing the crooked white cougar used incompetent Negrophobic Perjury to conceal Persecutory Negrophobia.

Your Majesty, what exactly is the point of Civil Procedure Rules, Statute, and Precedent - in Legal Systems where incompetent racist lies by white people, albeit only those prior agreed by members of the Antichrist closeted hereditary white supremacist Freemasonry Quasi-Religion (Mediocre Mafia, New Pharisees, New Good Samaritans, Defenders of Faiths, including all the Faiths associated with the 15 Holy Books in the House of Commons, and Dissenters of the Faith – John 14:6) are admissible – Habakkuk 1:4?

Your Majesty, crooked and incompetently dishonest GDC, Sue Gregory, Officer of the Most Excellent Order of our Empire (OBE), would have been in trouble had she been black, or had the Judges been black: White Privilege – Habakkuk 1:4.

CHAPTER FIVE: Dr Ngozi Ekweremadu, a Nigerian whistleblower

Case No: 2YL06820

Bedford County Court
May House
29 Goldington Road
Bedford
MK40 3NN

Monday, 1st July 2013

B E F O R E:

DISTRICT JUDGE AYERS

DOBERN PROPERTY LIMITED
(Claimants)

v.

DR. ABIODUN OLA BAMGBELU
(Defendant)

-

Transcript from an Official Court Tape Recording.

Transcript prepared by:
MK Transcribing Services
29 The Concourse, Brunel Business Centre,
Bletchley, Milton Keynes, MK2 2ES
Tel: 01908-640067 Fax: 01908-365958
DX 100031 Bletchley
Official Court Tape Transcribers.

MR. PURKIS appeared on behalf of THE CLAIMANTS.

THE DEFENDANT appeared in PERSON.

JUDGMENT

(As approved)

A verifiably very, very, sloppy Senior District Judge within one of the dullest adult populations in the industrialised world, among the least literate and the least numerate adults in the industrialised world – OECD.

"FAILING SCHOOLS AND A BATTLE FOR BRITAIN: This was the day the British education establishment's 50-year betrayal of the Nation's children lay starkly exposed in all its ignominy. After testing 166,000 people in 24 education systems, the Organisation for Economic Cooperation and Development (OECD) finds that England young adults are amongst the least literate and numerate in the industrialised world." Daily Mail, 09.01.2013

Young adults have LORDS.

LORDS of morons are likelier to be morons too.

Then, Lords knew that their sheep were morons, but sheep did not know that their Lords (shepherds) were morons too.

Sheep unnaturally shepherd sheep.

"Mediocrity weighing mediocrity in the balance, and incompetence applauding its brother." Wilde

Part of the resultant effects of several continuous centuries of stealing and Slavery – is that Britons, not all, are imbeciles (adults with the basic skills of a child), and an imbecile could become a postgraduate tutor in Great Britain, what's great about shit hole AFRICA?

"They may not have been well written from a grammatical point of view but I am confident I had not forgotten any of the facts." Geraint Evans of Rowtree Dental Care, , our Postgraduate Tutor, Oxford.

A CROOKED HEREDITARY RACIST WHITE WELSH IMBECILE.

NORTHAMPTON, ENGLAND: GDC, Geraint Evans, Postgraduate Tutor, Oxford, unrelentingly lied under implied oath (on record) – Habakkuk 1:4.

A very, very, dishonest white Welshman.

A closeted hereditary racist crooked Welsh bastard.

ACCURATE SEERS: They foresaw that a white Welsh imbecile will be our postgraduate tutor, Oxford, so they embarked on armed robbery and dispossession raids in our own Africa. Whenever the merciless armed racist bastards, and those they armed, sadistically slaughtered our own African ancestors, including the ancestors of Meghan Markle and her white children, they dispossessed them, and wherever they robbed Africans of their meagre possession, they took possession. Then, sadistic racist bastards were greedier than the grave, and like death, they were never satisfied – Habakkuk 2:5.

The report, by the OECD warns that the UK needs to take significant action to boost the basic skills of the nation's young people. The 460-page study is based on the first-ever survey of the literacy, numeracy and problem-solving at work skills of 16 to 65-year-olds in 24 countries, with almost 9,000 people taking part in England and Northern Ireland to make up the UK results. The findings showed that England and Northern Ireland have some of the highest proportions of adults scoring no higher than Level 1 in literacy and numeracy - the lowest level on the OECD's scale. This suggests that their skills in the basics are no better than that of a 10-year-old.

AN IMBECILE: AN ADULT WITH THE BASIC SKILLS OF A CHILD.

Then, all Judges were white, and most of them were Freemasons, and some of them were thicker than a gross of PLANKS, and white Freemason Judges who believed that daily dialogues with white imbeciles (predominantly but not exclusively white adults with the basic skills of a child) were worthwhile and manly – were scammers, and white Freemason Judges who demanded and accepted very, very, valuable considerations in exchange for daily dialogues with white imbeciles (predominantly but not exclusively white adults with the basic skills of a child) were racketeers (THIEVES) – Habakkuk 1:4.

What exactly is the point of civil procedure rules (cpr), statute, and precedent, in legal systems overseen by closeted hereditary white supremacist Masons, where white people, only white people, are allowed to tell lies - including under oath – Habakkuk 1:4, and where a Senior District Judge is verifiably dishonest, incompetent, and/or confused – Habakkuk 1:4?

Approved Judgments are accurate depiction of wilful statements of fact, so any deviation from the truth in an approved judgement must be a wilful dishonesty and/or malicious recklessness.

Your Majesty in Heaven, nearer our Father in Heaven, based on cogent, irrefutable, and available evidence, Bedford's District Judge Paul Robert Ayers, >70, a Mason, and the Senior Vice President of the Association of Her Majesty's District Judges of 3, St Paul's Square, MK 40 1SQ, maliciously lied, or was otherwise wilfully dishonest, or was recklessly confused - when he explicitly stated, in an approved Judgement – that a Negro from shit hole Africa, the only black person in the legal process, was invited to, and took part in a hearing at Bedford County Court, May House, 29 Goldington Road, Bedford, MK40 3NN, Monday, 1st July 2013.

The white man, albeit England's Class Senior Judge, LIED, or he was recklessly confused.

Google: The White Judge Lied.

Your Majesty in Heaven, nearer our Father in Heaven, what is left, when a Senior Judge, albeit England's Class, is verifiably thoroughly confused, or thoroughly incompetent, or indiscreetly and recklessly dishonest – Habakkuk 1:4?

OYINBO OLE (WHITE THIEVES): Nigerien children with gigantic uranium mines, and Nigerian children with huge oil wells and gas fields, near their huts, eat only 1.5/day in our own shit Africa, a brainless bellyful racist white bastard who white mother and father have never seen crude oil, and whose white ancestors, including ultra-righteous John Bunyan (1628 – 1688)

OXFORD, ENGLAND: Your Majesty in Heaven, nearer our Father in Heaven, based on cogent, irrefutable, and available evidence, GDC, British Soldier, Stephanie Twidale (Territorial Defence – TD), unrelentingly lied under oath – Habakkuk 1:4.

A very, very, dishonest white woman.

A racist crooked British Soldier.

What exactly was the point of civil procedure rules (cpr), statute, and precedent, in legal systems overseen by closeted hereditary white supremacist Masons, where a white closeted hereditary racist cougar, albeit a British Soldier (Territorial Defence) was allowed to, indiscreetly, audaciously, and unrelentingly, tell incompetent racist lies under oath – Habakkuk 1:4?

The USA is NATO, and absolutely everything else is an auxiliary bluff.

They are very, very, hardened intellectually incompetent racist white bastards, and they hate us, and we know.

New Herod, Matthew 2:16: They brainlessly and baselessly self-awarded supreme knowledge, and shallow and narrow hereditary closeted white supremacist bastards see molecules, and they destroy all Negurs, from shit hole AFRICA – who see atoms.

If there are cogent and irrefutable evidence that the white ancestors of the white father and mother of GDC, British Soldier, Stephanie Twidale (Territorial Defence – TD), were THIEVES and owners of stolen poor black children of defenceless Africans, including the African ancestors of

Meghan Markle's white children, it will be very, very, naïve, not to expect racial hatred complicated by incompetent mendacity to be part of her genetic inheritances – Habakkuk.

OYINBO OLE: An ignorant descendant of THIEVES and owners of stolen poor Negro children of defenceless Africans, including the African ancestors of Prince Harry's white children – Habakkuk.

Your Majesty, what exactly is the point of Civil Procedure Rules, Statute, and Precedent, in a Legal System whose entire foundation is built on incompetent decaying racist lies: The Decay of Lying – Wilde?

"Lies are told all the time." Sir Michael Havers (1923 – 1992).

Your Majesty, the pattern is the same almost everywhere.

If you disagree with the very, very, powerful members of the Antichrist Racist Freemasons (Mediocre Mafia, New Pharisees, New Good Samaritans, Defenders of Faiths, including all the exotic religions and faiths associated with the 15 Holy Books in the House of Commons, and Dissenters of the Faith – John 14:6), especially if you are a mere Negro from shit hole AFRICA, the closeted racist bastards will kill you, albeit hands-off.

Google: Dr Richard Bamgboye, GP.

They should rewrite their law: 'Freedom of expression for adults with the basic skills of a child (imbeciles)' should replace 'Freedom of Expression for all'.

Unlike her little brother, age saved the child's sister from the Closeted-Racist-Dylan–Roof-Freemason-Judge: Bedford's District Judge Paul Robert Ayers, >70, a Mason, and the Senior Vice President of the Association of Her Majesty's District Judges of 3, St Paul's Square, MK 40 1SQ.

She thanks her stars that the incontrovertibly functional semi-illiterate, closeted hereditary racist white man, Bedford's District Judge Paul Robert Ayers, >70, a Mason, and the Senior Vice President of the Association of Her Majesty's District Judges of 3, St Paul's Square, MK 40 1SQ, did not have anything to do with her education.

 In her GCSE, she gained the following grades:
English Language A*
English Literature A*
Mathematics A*
Additional Mathematics A*
Physics A*
Chemistry A*
Biology A*
History A*
Latin A
Spanish A

Advanced Level Mathematics A

Two years later, the child's sister, unimpeded by the closeted hereditary opportunist white supremacist former debt-collector Solicitor in Norwich (a mere poly-educated 5th rate partner), Bedford's District Judge Paul Robert Ayers, >70, a Mason, and the Senior Vice President of the Association of Her Majesty's District Judges of 3, St Paul's Square, MK 40 1SQ – gained 7 Grade A in the A/Level.

English	A
Mathematics	A
Chemistry	A
Latin	A
History	A
Biology	A
Critical Reasoning	A

Envy is a thief.
Indiscreet envy.

"Envy is weak." Yul Brynner.

The academic height that the white father and mother of the closeted racist white Bedford's District Judge Paul Robert Ayers, >70, a Mason, and the Senior Vice President of the Association of Her Majesty's District Judges of 3, St Paul's Square, MK 40 1SQ, CANNOT know, and which the natural talents of all his own white children will not exploit.

"Sometimes people don't want to hear the truth because they don't want their illusions destroyed." Friedrich Nietzsche

White supremacy and white privilege are con-joined twins, monsters with two heads, one body, two fertility tools, and four legs – travelling in the same direction.

White supremacy is real, and it needs to be shattered." Dr Cornel West.

"Meghan Markle was a subject of explicit and obnoxious racial hatred." John Bercow (a former speaker).

Meghan Markle is black because she is only 57% white. Michael Jackson was 100% white.

"Michael Jackson would have been found guilty if he'd been black." Jo Brand

The centuries-old unspoken myth that intellect is related to the universally acknowledged irrefutably superior skin colour that the very, very, fortunate wearer neither made nor chose, is mother of all racist scams.

"All men are created equal." Abraham Lincoln.

A liar.

"To the American founding fathers, the 'truth that all men are created equal' was 'self-evident'. It'd better be, for it certainly can't be proved. True equality can only exist in heaven; on earth, the belief that all men are created equal is wishful thinking. For men are created unequal in strength, intelligence, character – well, in everything. Earthly inequality is thus a natural order of things, and it can only be distorted by unnatural means. Even then it won't disappear; it'll be replaced by a worse type of inequality or else camouflaged by demagoguery." ALEXANDER BOOT, 2011.

The brain isn't skin colour; then, we were robbed with guns.

"It was our arms in the river of Cameroon, put into the hands of the trader, that furnished him with the means of pushing his trade; and I have no more doubt that they are British arms, put into the hands of Africans, which promote universal war and desolation that I can doubt their having done so in that individual instance. I have shown how great is the enormity of this evil, even on the supposition that we take only convicts and prisoners of war. But take the subject in another way, and how does it stand? Think of 80,000 persons carried out of their native country by we know not what means! For crimes imputed! For light or inconsiderable faults! For debts perhaps! For crime of witchcraft! Or a thousand other weak or scandalous pretexts! Reflect on 80,000 persons annually taken off! There is something in the horror of it that surpasses all bounds of imagination." – Prime Minister William Pitt the Younger

OYINBO OMO OLE: OYINBO OMO ALE.

The child sister has since gained a First-Class Science Degree from one of the topmost Universities in the UK, and she's gainfully engaged, batting for her Country.

The Negro from shit hole Africa is a British patriot.

Christ saved the child's sister from the evil clutches of the Closeted Racist Freemason Thugs (Mediocre Mafia, New Pharisees, New Good Samaritans, Defenders of Faiths, including all the exotic religions and faiths associated with the 15 Holy Books in the House of Commons, and Dissenters of the Faith – John 14:6) - Habakkuk 1:4.

It's plainly deductible that all the white children of Bedford's District Judge Paul Robert Ayers, >70, a Mason, and the Senior Vice President of the Association of Her Majesty's District Judges of 3, St Paul's Square, MK 40 1SQ, were inferiorly created by Almighty God, certainly intellectually - OECD.

https://www.youtube.com/watch?v=BlpH4hG7m1A.

If one were to ask the white man, albeit England's Class Senior Judge, to show one all his white children, and if he agrees, and if one were to ask his white children to hand-write short essays, and if they agreed, and if they could write legibly, Dr Richard Dawkins and OECD implied that they should be duller than their white father, a mere former debt collector Solicitor in Norwich and a High Ranking Functional Semi-illiterate Freemason (Scottish-Rite).

Our Prime Minister, the Edinburgh University Educated Scholar from Fife, couldn't spell; in a Country of the blind, the partially sighted is a Shepherd.

Re Meeting 9th March

Mon, 8 Mar 2010 20:20

George Rothnie georgerothnie@hotmail.comHide

To

Hi Ola,

We are scheduled to meet tomorrow evening at my surgery about 5.30ish. Unfortunately something has cropped up which necessytates me having to postpone the meeting. I'm really sorry it's such short notice.

I will contact you in the week to arrange another date.

Once agaim my apologies.

George.

A SCATTER-HEAD WHITE SCOTTISH IMBECILE, ALBEIT ENGLAND'S CLASS DEPUTY POSTGRADUATE DEAN, OXFORD.

CHAPTER SIX: Letter to the Sovereign, HM (1926 – 2022).

Case No: 2YL06820

Bedford County Court
May House
29 Goldington Road
Bedford
MK40 3NN

Monday, 1st July 2013

B E F O R E:

DISTRICT JUDGE AYERS

DOBERN PROPERTY LIMITED
(Claimants)

v.

DR. ABIODUN OLA BAMGBELU
(Defendant)

-

Transcript from an Official Court Tape Recording.
Transcript prepared by:

MK Transcribing Services
29 The Concourse, Brunel Business Centre,
Bletchley, Milton Keynes, MK2 2ES
Tel: 01908-640067 Fax: 01908-365958
DX 100031 Bletchley
Official Court Tape Transcribers.

MR. PURKIS appeared on behalf of THE CLAIMANTS.

THE DEFENDANT appeared in PERSON.

JUDGMENT
(As approved)

A verifiably very, very, sloppy Senior District Judge within one of the dullest adult populations in the industrialised world, among the least literate and the least numerate adults in the industrialised world – OECD.

"FAILING SCHOOLS AND A BATTLE FOR BRITAIN: This was the day the British education establishment's 50-year betrayal of the Nation's children lay starkly exposed in all its ignominy. After testing 166,000 people in 24 education systems, the Organisation for Economic Cooperation and Development (OECD) finds that England's young adults are amongst the least literate and numerate in the industrialised world." Daily Mail, 09.01.2013

Young adults have LORDS.

LORDS of morons are likelier to be morons too.

Lords know that their sheep are morons, but sheep do not know that Lords are morons too.

Sheep unnaturally shepherd sheep.

"Mediocrity weighing mediocrity in the balance, and incompetence applauding its brother." John 14:6

Part of the resultant effects of several continuous centuries of stealing and Slavery – is that Britons, not all, are imbeciles, and an imbecile could become a postgraduate tutor in Great Britain, what's great about that?

"They may not have been well written from a grammatical point of view but I am confident I had not forgotten any of the facts." Geraint Evans of Rowtree Dental Care, , our Postgraduate Tutor, Oxford.
A CROOKED HEREDITARY RACIST WHITE WELSH IMBECILE.

NORTHAMPTON, ENGLAND: GDC, Geraint Evans, Postgraduate Tutor, Oxford, unrelentingly lied under implied oath (on record) – Habakkuk 1:4.

A very, very, dishonest white Welshman.

A closeted hereditary racist crooked Welsh bastard.

ACCURATE SEERS: They foresaw that a white Welsh imbecile will be our postgraduate tutor, Oxford, so they embarked on armed robbery and dispossession raids in our own Africa. Whenever the merciless armed racist bastards, and those they armed, sadistically slaughtered our own African ancestors, including the ancestors of Meghan Markle and her white children, they dispossessed them, and wherever they robbed Africans of their meagre possession, they took possession. Then, sadistic racist bastards were greedier than the grave, and like death, they were never satisfied – Habakkuk 2:5.

The report, by the OECD warns that the UK needs to take significant action to boost the basic skills of the nation's young people. The 460-page study is based on the first-ever survey of the literacy, numeracy and problem-solving at work skills of 16 to 65-year-olds in 24 countries, with almost 9,000 people taking part in England and Northern Ireland to make up the UK results. The findings showed that England and Northern Ireland have some of the highest proportions of adults scoring no higher than Level 1 in literacy and numeracy - the lowest level on the OECD's scale. This suggests that their skills in the basics are no better than that of a 10-year-old.

AN IMBECILE: AN ADULT WITH THE BASIC SKILLS OF A CHILD. Then, all Judges were white, and most of them were Freemasons, and some of them were thicker than a gross of PLANKS, and white Freemason

Judges who believed that daily dialogues with white imbeciles (predominantly but not exclusively white adults with the basic skills of a child) were worthwhile and manly – were scammers, and white Freemason Judges who demanded and accepted very, very, valuable considerations in exchange for daily dialogues with white imbeciles (predominantly but not exclusively white adults with the basic skills of a child) were racketeers (THIEVES) – Habakkuk.

What exactly is the point of civil procedure rules (cpr), statute, and precedent, in legal systems overseen by closeted hereditary white supremacist Masons, where white people, only white people, are allowed to tell lies including under oath – Habakkuk 1:4, and where a Senior District Judge is verifiably dishonest, incompetent, and/or confused?

Approved Judgments are accurate depiction of wilful statements of fact, so any deviation from the truth in an approved judgement must be a wilful dishonesty and/or malicious recklessness.

Google: The White Judge Lied.

Your Majesty, based on cogent, irrefutable, and available evidence, Bedford's District Judge Paul Robert Ayers, >70, a Mason, and the Senior Vice President of the Association of Her Majesty's District Judges of 3, St Paul's Square, MK 40 1SQ, maliciously lied, or was otherwise wilfully dishonest, or was recklessly confused when he expressly stated, in an approved Judgement – that the African Negro, the only black person in the process, was invited to, and took part, in a hearing, at Bedford County Court, May House, 29 Goldington Road, Bedford, MK40 3NN, Monday, 1st July 2013.

Your Majesty, what is left, when a Senior Judge is verifiably thoroughly confused, or thoroughly incompetent, or indiscreetly and recklessly dishonest – Habakkuk 1:4?

OYINBO OLE (WHITE THIEVES): Nigerien children with gigantic uranium mines, and Nigerian children with huge oil wells and gas fields, near their huts, eat only 1.5/day in our own West Africa, a brainless bellyful racist white bastard who white mother and father have never seen crude oil, and whose white ancestors, including ultra-righteous John Bunyan (1628 – 1688)

OXFORD, ENGLAND: Your Majesty, based on cogent, irrefutable, and available evidence, GDC, British Soldier, Stephanie Twidale (Territorial Defence – TD), unrelentingly lied under oath – Habakkuk 1:4.

A very, very, dishonest white woman.

A racist crooked British Soldier.

What exactly was the point of civil procedure rules (cpr), statute, and precedent, in legal systems overseen by closeted hereditary white supremacist Masons, where a white closeted hereditary racist cougar was allowed to, indiscreetly, audaciously, and unrelentingly, tell incompetent racist lies under oath – Habakkuk 1:4?

The USA is NATO, and absolutely everything else is an auxiliary bluff.

They are very, very, hardened racist white bastards, and they hate us, and we know.

If there are cogent and irrefutable evidence that the white ancestors of the white father and mother of GDC, British Soldier, Stephanie Twidale (Territorial Defence – TD), were THIEVES and owners of stolen poor black children of defenceless Africans, including the African ancestors of Meghan Markle's white children, it will be very, very, naïve, not to expect racial hatred complicated by incompetent mendacity to be part of her genetic inheritances – Habakkuk.

OYINBO OLE: An ignorant descendant of THIEVES and owners of stolen poor Negro children of defenceless Africans, including the African ancestors of Prince Harry's white children – Habakkuk.

Your Majesty, what exactly is the point of Civil Procedure Rules, Statute, and Precedent, in a Legal System whose entire foundation is built on incompetent racist lies: The Decay of Lying – Wilde?

"Lies are told all the time." Sir Michael Havers (1923 – 1992).

The pattern is the same almost everywhere.

If you disagree with the Antichrist Racist Freemasons (Mediocre Mafia, New Pharisees, New Good Samaritans, Defenders of Faiths, including all the exotic religions and faiths associated with the 15 Holy Books in the House of Commons, and Dissenters of the Faith – John 14:6), especially if you are a mere Negro, from shit hole Africa, the closeted racist bastards will kill you, albeit hands-off.

Google: Dr Richard Bamgboye, GP.

White supremacy is real, and it needs to be shattered." Dr Cornel West.

"Meghan Markle was a subject of explicit and obnoxious racial hatred." John Bercow (a former speaker).

CHAPTER SEVEN: Dr Ngozi Ekweremadu, a Nigerian whistleblower

They're scared. The public must not know that intellect is absolutely unrelated to the universally acknowledged irrefutably superior skin colour that the very, very, fortunate wearer neither made nor chose.

England's young people are near the bottom of the global league table for basic skills. OECD finds 16- to 24-year-olds have literacy and numeracy levels no better than those of their grandparents' generation.

England is the only country in the developed world where the generation approaching retirement is more literate and numerate than the youngest adults, according to the first skills survey by the Organisation for Economic Co-operation and Development.

In a stark assessment of the success and failure of the 720-million-strong adult workforce across the wealthier economies, the economic thinktank warns that in England, adults aged 55 to 65 perform better than 16- to 24-year-olds at foundation levels of literacy and numeracy. The survey did not include people from Scotland or Wales.

The OECD study also finds that a quarter of adults in England have the maths skills of a 10-year-old. About 8.5 million adults, 24.1% of the population, have such basic levels of numeracy that they can manage only one-step tasks in arithmetic, sorting numbers or reading graphs. This is worse than the average in the developed world, where an average of 19% of people were found to have a similarly poor skill base.

Facts are sacred.

The pattern is the same almost everywhere in Great Britain, what's great about unashamed mediocrity and confusion?

NORTHAMPTON, ENGLAND: Based on available evidence, GDC-WITNESS, Dr Geraint Evans, Postgraduate Tutor, Oxford, unrelentingly lied under implied oath - Habakkuk 1:4; John 8:44; John 10:10.

A RACIST WHITE WELSH CROOK OF EMPIRE OF STOLEN AFFLUENCE: NEGROPHOBIC PERJURY GUIDES AND GUARDS PERSECUTORY NEGROPHOBIA – HABAKKUK 1:4.

"I am a free speech absolutist." Elon Musk.

BEDFORD: GDC, Richard Hill fabricated reports and unrelentingly lied under oath.

A Crooked Freemason.

A Dishonest Closeted Racist.

Antichrist Masonry: A Racist Scam.

"The best opportunity of developing academically and emotional." District Judge Paul Ayers of Bedford Court, 3, St Paul's Square MK401SQ, our Senior Vice President of the Association of Her Majesty's District Judges.

A brainless closeted hereditary racist white dunce.

White skin concealed a dark black brain.

Superior skin colour, stolen trust fund, and what else?

"I don't want to talk grammar. I want to talk like a lady." George Bernard Shaw (1856 – 1950).

Rishi Sunak: Masons teach members cultist-handshake, not grammar, and the former is considerably easier to master.

"All sections of UK society are institutionally racist." Sir Bernard Hogan-Howe.

Bedfordshire Police is part of UK society.

Apart from creating very, very, cushy salaried jobs for white semi-illiterate Solicitors and Barristers (predominantly but not exclusively white) who FAILED in practice, and loads did, why do white imbeciles (predominantly but not exclusively white adults with the basic skills of a child) need very, very, expensive administration of our law (quasi-communism)?

Our own Nigeria: Shell's docile cash cow since 1956.

Unlike Putin's Russia, there are no oil wells and gas field in Masons' Kempston and where the white mother and father of Bedford's District Judge Paul Robert Ayers, >70, a Mason, and the Senior Vice President of the Association of Her Majesty's District Judges of 3, St Paul's Square, MK 40 1SQ, were born.

Our own Urhobo babies, in our own shit hole Africa, with huge oil wells and gas fields near their huts eat only 1.5/day in our own NIGERIA, a very, very, bellyful, overfed, and overweight closeted hereditary racist semi-illiterate former debt-collector Solicitor in Norwich, a mere former 5th rate partner) whose white mummy and daddy have never seen crude oil, and whose white ancestors, including ultra-righteous John Bunyan (1628 – 1688), were fed like battery hens with yields of stolen poor black children of poor people, including the black African ancestors of Meghan Markle and her white children, was our Judge in Bedford, Great Britain, what's great about our hit hole AFRICA?

Facts are sacred.

Based on cogent, irrefutable, and available evidence, English law is equal for Caucasians and Africans, but its administration is not.

If all the White Master Builders (33rd Degree Freemasons - Scottish Rite), they're all white, at the Bedfordshire Masonic Temple to Baal, the Keep, Bedford Rd, Kempston, Bedford MK42 8AH, could prove that Bedford's District Judge Paul Robert Ayers, >70, a Mason, and the Senior Vice President of the Association of Her Majesty's District Judges of 3, St Paul's Square, MK 40 1SQ, was incontrovertibly a functional semi-illiterate, and an incompetent closeted Negrophobic perjurer, and if they could disprove the truth that the white man approved a sexed-up legal transcript, they will confirm the belief of scores of millions of white Britons (predominantly but not exclusively white), which is that sexed-up legal transcripts do not exist in the administration of English Law, and they will also confirm the belief of white Bedford's District Judge Paul Robert Ayers, >70, a Mason, and the Senior Vice President of the Association of Her Majesty's District Judges of 3, St Paul's Square, MK 40 1SQ, and his white spouse, which is that all their white children were not inferiorly created by Almighty God, certainly intellectually, and they will also confirm the belief of billions of people in our world, which is that Antichrist Freemasonry Quasi-Religion (Mediocre Mafia, New Pharisees, New Good Samaritans, Defenders of Faiths, including all the exotic faiths and religions associated with the 15 Holy Books in the House of Commons, and Dissenters of the Faith – John 14:6), Antichrist Islam, Antichrist Judaism, and all other motley assemblies of exotic religions and faiths under the Common Umbrella of the Governor of the Church of England and the Defender of the FAITH – John 14:6, are not intellectually flawed Satanic Mumbo Jumbo, and it will also confirm that reasoning and vision have boundaries, if reasoning and vision are finite, He must have lied when, before the Council, He disclosed pictures that His unbounded mind painted, and He must have also lied, when He audaciously stated: "I am the way and the truth and the life. No one comes to the Father except through me" (John 14:6).

If the fellow told the truth before the Council, everything that is not aligned to John 14:6 is travelling in the wrong direction and heading straight for very hard rocks.

"It does no harm to throw the occasional man overboard, but it does not do much good if you are steering full speed ahead for the rocks." Sir Ian Gilmour (1926 – 2007) Edinburgh University Educated, Dr George Rothnie, England's Class, Deputy Postgraduate Dean, Oxford.

Perception is grander than reality.

"Natural Selection will not remove ignorance from future generations." Dr Richard Dawkins.

They're scared. The public must not know that intellect is absolutely unrelated to the universally acknowledged irrefutably superior skin colour that the very, very, fortunate wearer neither made nor chose:Apartheid by stealth.

England's young people are near the bottom of the global league table for basic skills. OECD finds 16- to 24-year-olds have literacy and numeracy levels no better than those of their grandparents' generation.

England is the only country in the developed world where the generation approaching retirement is more literate and numerate than the youngest adults, according to the first skills survey by the Organisation for Economic Co-operation and Development.

In a stark assessment of the success and failure of the 720-million-strong adult workforce across the wealthier economies, the economic thinktank warns that in England, adults aged 55 to 65 perform better than 16- to 24-year-olds at foundation levels of literacy and numeracy. The survey did not include people from Scotland or Wales.

The OECD study also finds that a quarter of adults in England have the maths skills of a 10-year-old. About 8.5 million adults, 24.1% of the population, have such basic levels of numeracy that they can manage only one-step tasks in arithmetic, sorting numbers or reading graphs. This is worse than the average in the developed world, where an average of 19% of people were found to have a similarly poor skill base.

Facts are sacred.

The pattern is the same almost everywhere in Great Britain, what's great about unashamed mediocrity and confusion?

NORTHAMPTON, ENGLAND: Based on available evidence, GDC-WITNESS, Dr Geraint Evans, Postgraduate Tutor, Oxford, unrelentingly lied under implied oath - Habakkuk 1:4; John 8:44; John 10:10.

A RACIST WHITE WELSH CROOK OF EMPIRE OF STOLEN AFFLUENCE: NEGROPHOBIC PERJURY GUIDES AND GUARDS PERSECUTORY NEGROPHOBIA – HABAKKUK 1:4.

"I am a free speech absolutist." Elon Musk.

BEDFORD: GDC, Freemason, Brother Richard William Hill fabricated reports and unrelentingly lied under oath - Habakkuk 1:4.

A Crooked Freemason.

A Dishonest Closeted Racist.

Antichrist Masonry: A Racist Scam.

Bedford's District Judge Paul Robert Ayers, >70, a Mason, and the Senior Vice President of the Association of Her Majesty's District Judges of 3, St Paul's Square, MK 40 1SQ:Based on very proximate observations and direct experiences, you are physically and mentally ill-favoured by Almighty God. The mind that Divine Providence imposed, absolutely unsolicited, is considerably finer than the legal system you serve, and it is possible to employ cogent facts and irrefutable evidence to irreversibly destroy you and it.

"The best opportunity of developing academically and emotional." District Judge Paul Ayers of Bedford Court, 3, St Paul's Square MK401SQ, our Senior Vice President of the Association of Her Majesty's District Judges.

Sincere immodesty is sincerer than insincere modesty.

A brainless closeted hereditary opportunist racist white dunce: White skin concealed a dark black brain. Superior skin colour, stolen trust fund, and what else?

"I don't want to talk grammar. I want to talk like a lady." George Bernard Shaw (1856 – 1950).

Rishi Sunak: Masons teach members cultist-handshake, not grammar, and the former is considerably easier to master.

"All sections of UK society are institutionally racist." Sir Bernard Hogan-Howe.

Bedfordshire Police is part of UK society.

Apart from creating very, very, cushy salaried jobs for white semi-illiterate Freemason Solicitors and Barristers (predominantly but not exclusively white) who FAILED in practice, and loads did, why do white imbeciles (predominantly but not exclusively white adults with the basic skills of a child) need expensive administration of our law (quasi-communism)?

Our own Nigeria: Shell's docile cash cow since 1956.

Unlike Putin's Russia, there are no oil wells and gas field in Masons' Kempston and where the white mother and father of Bedford's District Judge Paul Robert Ayers, >70, a Mason, and the Senior Vice President of the Association of Her Majesty's District Judges of 3, St Paul's Square, MK 40 1SQ were born.

Our own Urhobo babies, in our own shit hole Africa, with huge oil wells and gas fields near their huts eat only 1.5/day, a very, very, bellyful, overfed, and overweight racist semi-illiterate former debt-collector Solicitor in Norwich whose white mummy and daddy have never seen crude oil, and whose white ancestors, including ultra-righteous John Bunyan (1628 – 1688), were fed like battery hens with yields of stolen children of poor people (African ancestors of Meghan Markle and her white children) is our Judge in Bedford, Great Britain, what's great about shit hole Africa?

Facts are sacred.

Based on cogent, irrefutable, and available evidence,
English law is equal for Caucasians and Africans, but its
administration is not.

If all the White Master Builders (33rd Degree Freemasons
- Scottish Rite), they're all white, at the Bedfordshire
Masonic Temple to Baal, the Keep, Bedford Rd,
Kempston, Bedford MK42 8AH, could prove
that Bedford's District Judge Paul Robert Ayers, >70, a
Mason, and the Senior Vice President of the Association of
Her Majesty's District Judges of 3, St Paul's Square, MK 40
1SQ, was incontrovertibly a functional semi-illiterate, and an
incompetent closeted Negrophobic perjurer, and if they could
disprove the truth that the white man approved a sexed-up
legal transcript, they will confirm the belief of scores of
millions of white Britons (predominantly but not exclusively
white), which is that sexed-up legal transcripts do not exist in
the administration of English Law, and they will also confirm
the belief of white Bedford's District Judge Paul Robert
Ayers, >70, a Mason, and the Senior Vice President of the
Association of Her Majesty's District Judges of 3, St Paul's
Square, MK 40 1SQ, and his white spouse, which is that
all their white children were not inferiorly created by
Almighty God, certainly intellectually, and they will also
confirm the belief of billions of people in our world, which
is that Antichrist Freemasonry Quasi-Religion (Mediocre
Mafia, New Pharisees, New Good Samaritans, Defenders
of Faiths, including all the exotic faiths and religions
associated with the 15 Holy Books in the House of
Commons, and Dissenters of the Faith – John 14:6),
Antichrist Islam, Antichrist Judaism, and all other motley

assemblies of exotic religions and faiths under the Common Umbrella of the Governor of the Church of England and the Defender of the FAITH – John 14:6, are not intellectually flawed Satanic Mumbo Jumbo, and it will also confirm that reasoning and vision have boundaries, if reasoning and vision are finite, He must have lied when, before the Council, He disclosed pictures that His unbounded mind painted, and He must have also lied, when He audaciously stated: "I am the way and the truth and the life. No one comes to the Father except through me" (John 14:6).

If the fellow told the truth before the Council, everything that is not aligned to John 14:6 is travelling in the wrong direction and heading straight for very hard rocks.

"It does no harm to throw the occasional man overboard, but it does not do much good if you are steering full speed ahead for the rocks." Sir Ian Gilmour (1926 – 2007).

CHAPTER EIGHT: Letter to the Sovereign, HM (1926 – 2022).

Google: Bedford: About 80,000, Predominantly, not Exclusively, Overfed White Fools.

Ian Brack, let me tell you, reasoning and vision have no finite boundaries, and the mind that Negro got, unsolicited, is considerably finer than the system you serve, and it is possible to use cogent facts and irrefutable evidence to irreversibly destroy it.

Ian Brack, are you a Mason?

We are all who we are, the inheritors of our inheritances, the genes of our individual ancestors, and only Divine Providence, the creator, deserves to suffer for the genetic characteristics, visible and invisible — that He imposed on His creations.

"The blame is his who chooses. God is blameless." Plato.

"A Welshman is a man who prays on his knees every Sunday and preys on his friends the rest of the week." English saying.

"They may not have been well written from a grammatical point of view but I am confident I had not forgotten any of the facts." Geraint Evans, Postgraduate Tutor, Oxford, of Rowtree Dental Care, Rowtree Road, Northampton NN4 0NY.

OYINBO ODE. OYINBO OLODO: OUR CROOKED RACIST WHITE WELSH IMBECILE POSTGRADUATE TUTOR, OXFORD, OF OUR EMPIRE OF STOLEN AFFLUENCE — HABAKKUK.

Our own Nigeria: Shell's docile cash cow since 1956. Based on available evidence, unlike Putin's Russia, there are no oil wells or gas fields in Wales, including Nick Griffin's Llanerfyl Powys, and where the white ancestors of the white mother and father of Geraint Evans, Postgraduate Tutor, Oxford, of Rowtree Dental Care, Rowtree Road, Northampton NN4 0NY, and the white ancestors of Aneurin Bevan (1897 - 1960), were born.

Our own Nigerian babies in our own shit hole AFRICA, with huge oil wells and gas fields near their huts eat only 1.5/day in our own NIGERIA, a very, very, bellyful, overfed, and overweight closeted hereditary racist white Welsh bastard whose white Welsh mother and father have never seen crude oil, and whose white Welsh ancestors, including the white Welsh ancestors of Aneurin Bevan (1897 – 1960), were fed like battery hens with gigantic yields of millions of stolen and defenceless poor black children of defenceless Africans, including the African ancestors of Meghan Markle and her white children - is our postgraduate tutor, Oxford, Great Britain; what's great about shit hole AFRICA?

Based on cogent, irrefutable, and available evidence, Aneurin Bevan's NHS was preceded by SLAVERY, and it paid for it. Ignorant descendants of THIEVES – Habakkuk.

Geraint Evans, white Welshman, let me tell you, you are very rich not because you are a fantastic dentist, you are rich only because you are a dentist in a very, very, rich Country (affluence was preceded by slavery), and because you are born in a relatively poor country that is fortunately near England. If Wales were to be detached from England at the River Severn, in Monmouthshire, and other boundary regions, she will be nearly as poor as Ukraine, the poorest Country in Europe.

Geraint Evans, based on cogent and irrefutable evidence, the white ancestors of your white mother and father were THIEVES and owners of stolen poor black children of defenceless Africans, including the black African ancestors of the great grandchildren of Prince Phillip (1921 - 2021).

Geraint Evans, are you a Mason?

Was Aneurin Bevan a Mason?

Philippians 1:21:

Was Phillip a 33rd Degree Mason, Scottish Rite?

Then, all the people of Wales were white, and all the sheep were white too, and nearly all Welsh Judges were closeted white supremacist Freemasons, and some of them were thicker than a gross of planks, and white Freemason Welsh Judges who had daily dialogues with white Welsh imbeciles (adults with the basic skills of a child), were expectedly, affected by their regular encounters, and they became very, very, dull.

Sir, Mr Justice Haddon-Cave, KC, KBE, apart from creating very, very, cushy salaried jobs for white Solicitors and Barristers (predominantly but not exclusively white) - who FAILED in practice, and loads did (quasi-communism), what do white imbeciles (predominantly but not exclusively white adults with the basic skills of a child) - need very, very, expensive administration of English Law for? It is plainly deductible that adults with the basic skills of a foetus will succeed adults with the basic skills of a child, and the former will need only food and shelter.

If Sir, Mr Justice Haddon-Cave, KC, KBE, could use cogent facts and irrefutable evidence to disprove the truth that his own imbecile white kindred, Geraint Evans, Postgraduate Tutor, Oxford, of Rowtree Dental Care, Rowtree Road, Northampton NN4 0NY, is not physically and intellectually ill-favoured by Almighty God, he will confirm the belief of Mrs Helen Falcon, Member of the Most Excellent Order of our Empire (MBE), a former member of the GDC

Committee, a very, very, charitable Rotarian (auxiliary Freemason), and the only spouse of Mr Falcon, which is that Geraint Evans, Postgraduate Tutor, Oxford, of Rowtree Dental Care, Rowtree Road, Northampton NN4 0NY, was not, generally, inferiorly created by Almighty God, and if all the 33rd Degree Freemason Judges in Great Britain, including at Cardiff Mason Hall, 8 Guildford St, Cardiff CF10 2HL, could disprove the truth, which is that Geraint Evans, Postgraduate Tutor, Oxford, of Rowtree Dental Care, Rowtree Road, Northampton NN4 0NY, unrelentingly lied under implied oath (on record) – Habakkuk 1:4, they will confirm the belief of billions of people in our common world, which is that Antichrist Freemasonry Quasi-Region (Mediocre Mafia, New Pharisees, New Good Samaritans, Defenders of Faiths, including all the exotic Faiths and Religions associated with the 15 Holy Books in the House of Commons, and Dissenters of the Faith - John 14:6), Antichrist Islam, Antichrist Judaism, and all other motley assemblies of Faiths and Religions under the common umbrella of the Governor of the Church of England and the Faith - John 14:6, our own faith, and only our faith, are not intellectually flawed Satanic Mumbo Jumbo, and they will also confirm that reasoning and vision have finite boundaries, and reasoning and vision have fin ite boundaries, the fellow must have LIED to Jews and Romans, when, in the Council, He disclosed pictures His unbounded mind painted, and He must have also LIED - when with arrogant audacity He openly declared that He was above all, and extraordinarily exceptional - John 14:6.

"Freedom of Expression is a basic right." Lady Hale

Freedom of Expression was part of the last Queen Speeches (1926 - 2022).

Whenever HM the King - raises the bar of freedom to disclose pictures painted by free minds, including for Negurs from shit hole Africa - to the level that was acceptable to President Thomas Jefferson (1743 – 1826), very, very, charitable Freemasonry Quasi-Religion will be uncovered and irreversibly destroyed, and it will be in the public interest - as part of the face of the exceptional fellow, the only transparently true Judge - who will judge all, including crooked closeted white supremacist Freemason Judges - with the transparent sword of truth, not Jonathan Aitken's, the only real one, will be concomitantly uncovered for all to see - John 5:22, Matthew 25:31 - 46, and John 14:6.

"There is not a truth existing which I fear or would wish unknown to the whole world." President Thomas Jefferson (1743 – 1826)

Based on cogent, irrefutable, and available evidence, very, very charitable Freemasonry Quasi-Religion – is a centuries-old elaborate white supremacists' scam.

New Herod. Matthew 2;16: Thoroughly deluded, ignorant, and hereditary closeted white supremacist bastards see molecules, and they use incompetent racist mendacity to destroy all Negurs from shit hole AFRICA - who see atoms.

Based on several decades of very, very, proximate observations and direct experiences, the white man is grossly overrated.

"He is an Englishman, usually violent and always dull."
Wilde

Helen Falcon, MBE: Our overpromoted, closeted hereditary racist mere dmf. A racist descendant of THIEVES and owners of stolen children of poor people, including the black African ancestors of Meghan Markle and her white children - Habakkuk. An ultra-righteous and super-enlightened Member of the Most Excellent Order of our Empire of Stolen Affluence - Habakkuk.

Ignorance is bliss.

"Those who know least obey the best." George Farquhar.

OYINBO OMO OLE: OYINBO OMO ALE - HABAKKUK.

Google: Helen Falcon, Racist Empress of Privileged Dullards.

Sir, Mr Justice Haddon-Cave, KBE, KC, your own white kindred, Geraint Evans, Postgraduate Tutor, Oxford, of Rowtree Dental Care, Rowtree Road, Northampton NN4

0NY employed your own language, not ours, like an imbecile ashawo – a prostitute with the basic skills of a child) from oil and gas rich Nigeria - who is in Great Britain to study symmetrical eyebrows decoration.

Sir, Mr Justice Haddon-Cave KC, KBE, based on available evidence, unlike Putin's Russia, there are no oil wells or gas fields where your own white mother and father were born, and the white ancestors of your own white mother and father, including the white ancestors of unapologetic white supremacist, Sir Winston Churchill (1874–1965), were fed like battery hens with yields of millions of stolen poor black children of defenceless Africans, including the black African ancestors of Meghan Markle and her white children - Habakkuk.

Facts are sacred.

"The truth allows no choice." Dr Samuel Johnson

Based on cogent, irrefutable, and available evidence, the Royal Courts of Justice, Strand, London WC2A 2LL, were preceded by the extortionately profitable, very greedy, racist, crude, and cruel commerce in carrying and selling millions of stolen human beings, including the black African ancestors of Meghan Markle and white children, and the yields of several centuries of merciless racist evil paid for the Grand Cathedral Courts.

Facts are sacred.

"Those who know the least obey the best." George Farquhar.

Omo ale ti ko gbo ede awon Baba nla re.

Awon ari teni moowi, afi apadi bo ti won mole.

Sir, Mr Justice Haddon-Cave, KBE, KC, if it could be
disproved that your own white kindred, Geraint Evans,
Postgraduate Tutor, Oxford, of Rowtree Dental Care,
Rowtree Road, Northampton NN4 0NY was a closeted
hereditary racist crooked white imbecilic bastard, it will
confirm that the Nigerian is a lunatic.

No brain.

Unlike Putin's Russia, there are no oil wells or gas fields in
Wales, including in Nick Griffin Llanerfyl Powys.

Several centuries of stealing and slavery preceded the
gigantic stolen trust fund - Habakkuk.

Only their universally acknowledged irrefutably superior
skin colour and God Almighty are truly good — Mark 10:18,
and they neither made nor chose it, and they will be

considerably diminished as human beings without it, and they know it.

Ignorant descendants of ultra-righteous white thieves and owners of stolen poor black children of defenceless Africans, including the black African ancestors of Meghan Markle and her white children.

Part of the enduring residues of several continuous centuries of very, very, civilised and super-enlightened European Christians' commerce in millions of stolen poor black African children, including the African ancestors of Meghan Markle and her white children: Based on several decades of very, very, proximate observations and direct experiences, some white privileged dullards find it very, very, difficult to accept the truth, which is that intellect is a function of genetic mix, and it is the exclusive preserve of Almighty God, and it is absolutely unrelated to their universally acknowledged irrefutably superior skin colour, which the very, very, fortunate wearer neither made nor chose, and some self-educated Africans are, by far, intellectually superior to some white privileged dullards (predominantly but not exclusively white).

Sincere immodesty is sincerer than insincere modesty.

New Herod, Matthew 2:16: Ian Brack, some brainless white privileged dullards (predominantly but not exclusively white) see molecules, and they destroy all self-educated Africans who secretly look down on their mediocre, shallow, and myopic intellects, and see atoms.

Ian Brack, the Negro does not fit into your mediocre and indiscreetly institutionally racist system, not by choice, but by genetic makeup.

WE DISAGREE WITH CLOSETED HEREDITARY WHITE SUPREMACIST BASTARDS.

"To disagree with three – fourths of the British public on all points is one of the first elements of sanity, one of the deepest consolations in all moments of spiritual doubt." Wilde.

Before Slavery, what?

Prior to SLAVERY, their thoroughly wretched white ancestors, barbarian, rabbit hunters, and mere agricultural labourers — worked with forks and spades on the estates of landowners (stolen land).

"It was in 1066 that William the Conqueror occupied Britain, stole our land, and gained control of it by granting it to his Norman, hence the feudal system that we have not yet fully escaped." Tony Benn, multi-millionaire quasi-communist (1925–2014).

William the Conqueror stole from others what others stole from others.

"All have taken what had other owners and all have had recourse to arms rather than quit the prey onto which they were fastened." Dr Samuel Johnson.

GDC: Geraint Evans (NHS Postgraduate Tutor), unrelentingly lied under oath (on record) — Habakkuk 1:4.

A very, very, dishonest white Welsh man.

Our crooked closeted hereditary racist Helen Falcon's NHS Postgraduate Tutor of our Empire of Stolen Affluence — Habakkuk.

They are inferiorly intellectually created by Almighty God, and they know, and to conceal that that truth they resort to incompetent mendacious criminality, and the weapon of the direct descendants of the father of lies (John 8:44) is the mother of racist lies, and their power is the certainty that all Judges will be white, and their hope is that all Judges will be closeted hereditary white supremacist bastards too – Habakkuk 1:4.

It plainly deductible that GDC, Geraint Evans (NHS Postgraduate Tutor) was lied to at home by his white Welsh mother and father, and at school, by his white Welsh teachers

— that it was his birth right to be superior to all Africans, and when, in the real world, he realised his white Welsh mother, father, and his teachers LIED to him, he resorted to indiscreet racist criminality, and his safety was that Judges will be white, and his hope was that they will be closeted white supremacist bastards too — Habakkuk 1:4.

If there is cogent and irrefutable evidence that one's Welsh ancestors were THIEVES and owners of stolen poor black children of defenceless Africans, including the black African ancestors of the white niece and nephew of the Prince of Wales, it will be very, very, naive not to expect RACIAL HATRED, complicated by incompetent mendacity to be part of one's genetic inheritances — Habakkuk.

OXFORD, ENGLAND: GDC, Bristol University Educated Mrs Helen Falcon, Member of the Most Excellent Order of our Empire (MBE), a former member of the GDC Committee, a Rotarian (auxiliary Freemason), a former Postgraduate Dean, Oxford, and the only spouse of Mr Falcon, unrelentingly lied under oath (on record) — Habakkuk 1:4.

A very, very, dishonest crooked racist white cougar, and an ignorant Member of the Most Excellent Order of our Empire of Stolen Affluence — Habakkuk.

Based on available evidence, the entire foundation of Bristol, including Bristol University where the crooked hereditary racist cougar studied softish dentistry, was built with bones, bones of stolen poor black children of defenceless Africans, including the African ancestors of Meghan Markle and her white children, and more bones than the millions of skulls at the doorstep of Comrade Pol Pot (1925–1998).

CHAPTER NINE: Dr Ngozi Ekweremadu, a Nigerian whistleblower.

Ian Brack, based on several decades of very, very, proximate observations and direct experiences, before the RACIAL HATRED of closeted hereditary white supremacist privileged dullards unravel, it is always a conspiracy theory, and when it does, it instantly mutates to a mistake.

"The white man is the devil." Mohammed Ali (1942–2016).

Their hairs stand on end when they are challenged by Negroes from shit hole Africa, we and our type are the ones closeted hereditary white supremacist bastards will beat up without the support of the YANKS.

Skin colour that they neither made nor chose is universally acknowledged to be irrefutably superior, but their intellects aren't, and their legal system is fundamentally designed to conceal that TRUTH.

Superiority is their brainless and baseless birth right, and they love their universally acknowledged irrefutably superior skin colour that they neither made nor chose, but they HATE Freedom of Expression because they don't want their mentally children to know that they are not SUPERIOR.

Based on several decades of very, very, proximate observations and direct experiences, they are more impervious to other views than lunatic Jihadists, and like Putin, Kim, MBS, and Babies, they expect all Negroes from shit hole Africa to love them unconditionally, and they, very arrogantly, baselessly, and brainlessly self-awarded supreme knowledge, and they expect all our people to see our common world only from the perspective of members of the self-awarded superior race, and they expect all Negroes from shit hole Africa to say, write, and/or print only what members of the self-awarded superior race love to hear: New Herod.

Matthew 14: The intolerant lunatic Jew, King Herod, jailed John only because he spoke what he did not love to hear, and he removed his head solely to permanently prevent him from speaking.

The last decapitation with an axe in Great Britain was in 1817, and decapitation was removed from the Statute book in 1973, and in the same year, Kenneth Baker banned flogging in Schools.

"There is now less flogging in our great schools than formerly, but then less is learned there; so that what the boys get at one end, they lose at the other." Dr Samuel Johnson.

BEDFORD, ENGLAND: District Judge Paul Robert Ayers, >70, a Mason, and the Senior Vice President of the

Association of Her Majesty's District Judges of 3, St Paul's Square, MK 40 1SQ, which part of our Bedfordshire Masonic Centre, the Keep, Bedford Road, Kempston, MK42 8AH, wasn't stolen, or which part of it is the yield of the Higher IQs of your own white mother and father, or which part of it preceded SLAVERY: The Grand building (Territorial Defence) or its chattels?

Ignorance is bliss.

"I do not approve of anything that tampers with natural ignorance. Ignorance is like a delicate exotic fruit; touch it and the bloom is gone. The whole theory of modern education is radically unsound. Fortunately, in England, at any rate, education produces no effect whatsoever. If it did, it would prove a serious danger to the upper classes, and probably lead to acts of violence in Grosvenor Square." Wilde.

When it became apparent that the fellow was intellectually unplayable, and the Divine Magician was 'stealing' their crowd, BUILDERS stitched him up, and lynched Him like Gadhafi, and He was crucified only because He spoke; He disclosed pictures His unbounded mind painted. They fellow was not punished for speaking — by intolerant bastards, He was lynched like Gadhafi and crucified solely to prevent Him from speaking.

The stone that the BUILDERS rejected is now the cornerstone — Psalm 118:22, Luke 20:17.

CONFLICT OF INTEREST: It is plainly deductible that those who nominated and appointed Mrs Helen Falcon (MBE), our very, very, dishonest racist white cougar, and our ignorant, crooked, and closeted hereditary white supremacist Member of the Most Excellent Order of our Empire of Stolen Affluence — Habakkuk, are culpable, and they sit in Judgement in disputes involving a mere Negro from shit hole Africa, and their appointee, Mrs Helen Falcon, an accurate reflection of the very, very, powerful privileged dullards, almost certainly Freemasons, who appointed her.

Google: Mediocre Great England.

Ian Brack, all these were before your time, but the pattern is the same almost everywhere in Great Britain.

"All sections of UK society are institutionally racist." Sir Bernard Hogan — Howe.

GDC is part of UK society. Ian Brack, based on several decades of very, very, proximate observations and direct experiences, closeted hereditary white supremacist privileged dullards are intellectually wonky, and they are psychologically and intellectually insecure.

Nigerien and Nigerian children with huge uranium mines and/or crude oil and gas fields near their huts eat only 1.5/day in our own shit hole Africa, a very, very, bellyful homunculus hereditary racist white cougar, Mrs Helen Falcon (MBE), whose white father and mother have never seen crude oil, and whose mentally gentler children might not be able to spell uranium, and whose white ancestors, including the white ancestors of Aneurin Bevan (1897–1960), were fed like battery hens with yields of millions of stolen poor black children of defenceless Africans, including the African ancestors of Meghan Markle and her white children, a mere dmf, was a Member of our GDC Committee, and our Postgraduate Dean Oxford.

Aneurin Bevan's NHS was preceded by SLAVERY, and it paid for it.

Facts are sacred, and they cannot be overstated.

ACCURATE SEERS: Then, the white ancestors of the white mother and father of GDC, Bristol University Educated Mrs Helen Falcon, Member of the Most Excellent Order of our Empire (MBE), a former member of the GDC Committee, a Rotarian (auxiliary Freemason), a former Postgraduate Dean, Oxford, and the only spouse of Mr Falcon, foresaw that she will be talentless, but become somebody in Great Britain, so they embarked on armed robbery and dispossession raids in AFRICA, and whenever the very, very, very, greedy, and armed racist bastards, and those they armed — mercilessly slaughtered unarmed Africans, including the black African

ancestors of Meghan Markle and her white children, they
dispossessed them, and wherever they robbed Africans of
their meagre possessions, they took possession of what had
other owners. They were THIEVES, and Helen Falcon
(MBE) is a THIEF, but only by heritage.

Then, the white ancestors of the white mother and father of
GDC, Bristol University Educated Mrs Helen Falcon,
Member of the Most Excellent Order of our Empire (MBE),
a former member of the GDC Committee, a Rotarian
(auxiliary Freemason), a former Postgraduate Dean, Oxford,
and the only spouse of Mr Falcon, were greedier than the
grave, and like death, the armed racist bastards were never
satisfied — Habakkuk 2:5.

Now, GDC, Bristol University Educated Mrs Helen Falcon,
Member of the Most Excellent Order of our Empire (MBE),
a former member of the GDC Committee, a Rotarian
(auxiliary Freemason), a former Postgraduate Dean, Oxford,
and the only spouse of Mr Falcon, and her type — fear the
untamed minds of self-educated Negurs, from shit hole
Africa, more than Putin's poisons.

Ian Brack, then the armed white ancestors of the white
mother and father of GDC, Bristol University Educated Mrs
Helen Falcon, Member of the Most Excellent Order of our
Empire (MBE), a former member of the GDC Committee, a
Rotarian (auxiliary Freemason), a former Postgraduate Dean,
Oxford, and the only spouse of Mr Falcon, and her type, and

those they armed, stalked Africans like prey, in the African bush, and like wild dogs, they hunted in packs.

"There is no hunting like the hunting of man, and those who have hunted armed men long enough and liked it, never care for anything else thereafter." Ernest Hemingway (1899–1961).

Ian Brack, dentistry (dmf) is one of the softest sciences, and based on very, very, proximate observations and direct experiences, it is not manly.

It is not the truth that what a man can do, a woman can do, and it is not the truth that men should do easier jobs that women can do.

Then, there were no women palm wine tappers in our tribe in the West African bush.

In the distant future, only women and she-she-men will be allowed to practice very, very, soft Nursing and Dentistry.

Ian Brack, based on cogent and irrefutable evidence, it is absolutely impossible for GDC, Bristol University Educated Mrs Helen Falcon, Member of the Most Excellent Order of our Empire (MBE), a former member of the GDC Committee, a Rotarian (auxiliary Freemason), a former Postgraduate Dean, Oxford, and the only spouse of Mr

Falcon, and her type, crooked hereditary closeted white supremacist bastards — to compete on a level, colour-blind intellectually playing field — without resorting to racist criminality guided and guarded by incompetent mendacity — Habakkuk 1:4.

They desired intellectual superiority, but the creator gave them superior skin colour, and in protest, closeted hereditary white supremacist bastards stole what He gave Negurs from shit hole Africa - Habakkuk.

Ian Brack, the centuries-old unspoken myth that intellect is related to the universally acknowledged irrefutably superior skin colour that the very, very, fortunate wearer neither made nor chose.

OXFORD, ENGLAND: GDC, British Soldier, Stephanie Twidale (TD), unrelentingly lied under oath — Habakkuk 1:4.

A very, very, dishonest white woman.

Our hereditary racist crooked British Soldier, albeit Territorial Defender.

The USA is NATO, and absolutely everything else is an auxiliary bluff.

"England will fight to the last American." American saying.

Ian Brack, if you could disprove the truth that OXFORD, ENGLAND: GDC, British Soldier, Stephanie Twidale (TD), unrelentingly lied under oath — Habakkuk 1:4, and if you could disprove the truth that OXFORD, ENGLAND: GDC, Bristol University Educated Mrs Helen Falcon, Member of the Most Excellent Order of our Empire (MBE), a former member of the GDC Committee, a Rotarian (auxiliary Freemason), a former Postgraduate Dean, Oxford, and the only spouse of Mr Falcon, unrelentingly lied under oath (on record) — Habakkuk 1:4, you will confirm the belief of all white privileged dullards in Great Britain (predominantly but not exclusively white), and all the white 33rd Degree Freemasons (Scottish Rite) at Bedfordshire Masonic Centre, the Keep, Bedford Road, Kempston, MK42 8AH, and all the white 33rd Degree Freemasons — Scottish Rite (predominantly but not exclusively white) at the Grand Masonic Temple (the Mother Lodge), 60 Great Queen Street, London WC2B 5AZ, which is that Antichrist Freemasonry Quasi-Religion (Mediocre Mafia, New Pharisees, New Good Samaritans, Defenders of Faiths, including all the motley assemblies of exotic faiths and religions associated with all the 15 Holy Books in the House of Commons, and Dissenters of the Faith — John 14:6), Antichrist Islam, Antichrist Judaism, and all the motley assemblies of exotic religions and faiths under the common umbrella of the Governor of the Church of England and the Defender of the Faith — John 14:6, are not intellectually flawed Satanic Mumbo Jumbo, and it will also confirm that reasoning and vision have finite boundaries, and if reasoning and vision have finite boundaries, He must have lied when He disclosed pictures His unbounded mind painted, and He must have also lied when He explicitly declared that He extraordinarily exceptional — John 14:6. White privileged dullards (predominantly but not exclusively white) are racist white bastards and criminals, and the weapon of the direct descendants of the father of lies (John 8:44) is the mother of racist lies, and their power is the certainty that all Judges will be white, and their hope is that all Judges will closeted hereditary white supremacist bastards too.

Based on several decades of very, very, proximate observations and direct experiences, homogeneity in the administration of English law is the impregnable secure mask of merciless racist evil - Habakkuk 1:4.

CHAPTER TEN: Letter to the Sovereign, HM (1926 – 2022)

"**Of** black men, the numbers are too great who are now repining under English cruelty." Dr Samuel Johnson.

2 Thessalonians 3:6-10: A brainless racist white bastard. Then, everyone was white, and all white District Judges sent their white universities - to gain qualifications so that they can eat their own food, and more importantly, to use their sensuous putrid tubes to ensnare men who would pay them for insertion – Quasi-prostitution.

Which one of our putrid tubes did our Born-Again Christian tell Bedford's District Judge and Masons at Brickhill Baptist Church she used to work for £0.5M?

"The best opportunity of developing academically and emotional." Bedford's District Judge Paul Robert Ayers, >70, a Mason, and the Senior Vice President of the Association of Her Majesty's District Judges of 3, St Paul's Square, MK 40 ısǫ: A brainless closeted hereditary white supremacist bastard.

Superior skin colour concealed a dark black brain.

No brain.

Poor in natural resources: Unlike Putin's Russia, there are no oil wells or gas fields where his own white mother and father were born.

Several continuous centuries of stealing and slavery preceded the GIGANTIC stolen trust fund – Habakkuk.

Only his universally acknowledged irrefutably superior skin colour and Almighty God are truly good – Mark 10:18, and he neither made nor chose it, and he will be considerably diminished as a human being without it, and he knows it.

Skin colour is a great creation of Almighty God, but it is not the greatest.

Then, and only there, when their people committed racist crimes against ours, their people who oversaw the administration of their institutionally racist law (closeted hereditary white supremacist Freemason Judges), criminally buried RACIAL HATRED, and they did everything legally — under Civil Procedure Rules, Statute, and Precedent.

THE WHITE JUDGE STANK.

Based on contacts, Bedford's District Judge Paul Robert Ayers, >70, a Mason, and the Senior Vice President of the Association of Her Majesty's District Judges of 3, St Paul's Square, MK 40 1SQ, had a distinct body odour, the white man, a Briton, stank.

"Britons stank." W.S.

Wole Soyinka, not William Shakespeare should know, as one of his wives and some of his concubines were Britons.

Some Britons are Jews.

"American Airlines insisted the reason it kicked the family off the plane was their scent and not because they are Jewish. "The Adler family were asked to deplane last night after several passengers, along with our crew members, complained about their body odour," American Airlines said in a statement." News.

Irish Catholic Joe, how much money did your ancestors have in their pockets when they disembarked on stolen Indian land?

How come only 1.4% of Americans are Jews, and 50% of the billionaires in America are Jews?

Then, when they FU*KED, which was often, genius Jews were their GO-TO-PEOPLE.

It is a brainless and baseless myth that all Jews are geniuses (Albert Einstein).

There are imbeciles everywhere in the world.

"Jews are intelligent and creative, Chinese are intelligent but not creative, Indians are servile, and Africans are morons." Professor James Watson (DNA) paraphrased.

A dementing genetic Scot.

Alzheimer's disease is considerably more common than ordinarily realised, and it is colour-blind.

Then, very, very, greedy racist white bastards knew how to steal money for their own white kindred, but they didn't know how to repair the scatter-heads of closeted hereditary white supremacist bastards.

Then, very, very, greedy racist white bastards used guns to steal for their own white kindred, and they carried and sold

millions of stolen poor black children of defenceless
Africans, including African ancestors of Meghan Markle and
her white children, now, they steal our own natural resources
from our own Africa.

Substitution is not emancipation; it is fraudulent deceit.

"Moderation is a virtue only among those who are thought to
have alternatives." Henry Kissinger.

"How Europe underdeveloped Africa." Dr Walter Rodney
(1942–1980).

If we aren't very, very, smart, why are we very, very, rich?

Then, everyone was white.

Shepherds didn't bring stolen African children home, they
lied to their mentally gentler children that they were paragons
of wisdom and virtue who, like Mother Teresa of Calcutta,
did only very, very, good works in AFRICA.

"It was our arms in the river of Cameroon, put into the hands
of the trader, that furnished him with the means of pushing
his trade; and I have no more doubt that they are British
arms, put into the hands of Africans, which promote
universal war and desolation that I can doubt their having
done so in that individual instance. I have shown how great is

the enormity of this evil, even on the supposition that we take only convicts and prisoners of war. But take the subject in another way, and how does it stand? Think of 80,000 persons carried out of their native country by, we know not what means! For crimes imputed! For light or inconsiderable faults! For debts perhaps! For the crime of witchcraft! Or a thousand other weak or scandalous pretexts! Reflect on 80,000 persons annually taken off! There is something in the horror of it that surpasses all bounds of imagination." — Prime Minister William Pitt the Younger.

"The white man is the devil." Elijah Mohammed (1897–1975).

Based on several decades of very, very, proximate observations and direct experiences, the white man is not just the devil, he is also a THIEF.

BEDFORD, ENGLAND: GDC, Freemason, Brother, Richard William Hill (NHS Postgraduate Tutor), unrelentingly lied under oath.

A very, very, dishonest white man.

A closeted hereditary white supremacist Freemason crooked NHS Postgraduate Tutor of our Empire of Stolen Affluence — Habakkuk.

Had he been black, or had the Judges been black, he would have been in trouble.

Only stupid black people (Africans) expect Caucasians to voluntarily relinquish several continuous centuries of advantageous positions in exchange for NOTHING, and only stupider Negroes expect closeted hereditary white supremacist Freemason Judges to measure shit hole Africans with the same yardstick they use to measure their own white kindred, and only the stupidest among Africans expect demons to cast out demons — Matthew 12:27.

"Sometimes people don't want to hear the truth because they don't want their illusions destroyed." Friedrich Nietzsche.

Matthew 19:21: He ordered the very, very, rich Jew to sell all the yields of transparent virtue, give all the proceeds to the poor, and follow him; the very, very, rich Jew disobeyed the order of the only true Judge — John 5:22, Matthew 25: 31–46.

He orders inheritors of yields of several continuous centuries of stolen and destroyed lives to return yields of industrial-scale organised stealing, they disobey the clear order.

BEDFORD, ENGLAND: District Judge Paul Robert Ayers, >70, a Mason, and the Senior Vice President of the Association of Her Majesty's District Judges of 3, St Paul's Square, MK 40 1SQ,, let me tell you, equitable and just reparation pend, and centuries of unpaid interest accrue, if your own white mother and father did not tell you all those, they lied to you.

Our functional semi-illiterate racist white bastard. Our direct descendant of ultra-righteous white professional thieves and owners of stolen poor black children of defenceless Africans, including the black African ancestors of Meghan Markle and her white children.

BEDFORD, ENGLAND: District Judge, which part of our County Court, 3, St Paul's Square, MK40 1SQ, wasn't stolen, or which part of it is the yield of the Higher IQs of your own white mother and father, or which part of it did transparent virtue yield, or which part of it did our good people of Bedford buy, or which part of it preceded SLAVERY: The building or its chattels?

A closeted hereditary racist descendant of ultra-righteous white THIEVES and owners of stolen poor black children of defenceless AFRICANS, including the African ancestors of Meghan Markle and her white children — Habakkuk.

OYINBO OMO OLE: OYINBO OMO ALE.

"We are just an advanced breed of monkeys on a minor planet of a very average star. But we can understand the Universe. That makes us something very special." Dr Stephen Hawking (1942–2018).

Prime Minister Benjamin Disraeli (1804–1881) was born during the European Christians' extortionately profitable, very, very, crude, and sadistically cruel commerce in millions of stolen poor black children of defenceless Africans, including the African ancestors of Meghan Markle and white children.

The white ancestors of Prime Minister Benjamin Disraeli did not evolve from black monkeys with tails to tailless white monkeys in the Epping Forest.

Based on available evidence, gigantic yields of millions of stolen poor black African children, not feudal agriculture, lured Jews, including the white ancestors of Benjamin Disraeli to Great Britain.

Jews followed the money: Yields of millions of stolen and destroyed lives.

Properly rehearsed ultra-righteousness and deceptively schooled civilised decorum were preceded by several continuous centuries of merciless racist evil: The greediest economic cannibalism and the evilest racist terrorism the world will ever know — Habakkuk.

Then, very, very, greedy racist white bastards were greedier than the grave, and like death, they were never satisfied — Habakkuk 2:5.

Now, they are very, very, highly civilised and super-enlightened, so they use incompetent racist lies, not guns, to steal for the benefit of their own white kindred — Habakkuk 1:4.

CHAPTER ELEVEN: Dr Ngozi Ekweremadu, a Nigerian
Whistleblower

"This statement is about a series of letters and emails I have
been recieving. I am the above named person. I live at an
address provided to police. In this statement I will also
mention XXXXXXXXXXXXXXXXXXXXXXXXXXXX a
leaseholder for a property I manage at my place work. I am
the company director of DOBERN properties based in Ilford.
These emails have been sent to my company email address
of mail@debern.co.uk, and also letters have been sent to
myself at our company ADDress of P.O BOX 1289,
ILFORD, IG2 7XZ over the last Two and a half years, I have
recieving a series of letters and emails from DR BAMGeLu.
DR BAMGBELU is a leasholder for a property I manage at
my place of work. Over the period of his leaseholding, DR
BAmGelu has continually failed to pay arrears for the
property. In march 2016 my company took DR to court and
he was ordered to pay outstanding costs of around £20000
since that time and lead up to the case, DR BaMGBelu has
been emailing me and posting me letters that are lengthy and
accuses me repeatedly of being a racist in emails and letters
tact are regularly Ten to twelve pages long, DR
BAMGBELU. lists numerous quots from google searches all
refrencing ham I am a bigot and a racist. The most recent
letter I received from DR BAMGBELU opens with you are
jealous and racist Evil combination you hate us we know it"
he goes on to say "I would not have knowingly had anything

to do with white supremicists." In the last email I recieved from him on 02/09/2016 DR BaMGBELU stated "you are restricted by poor Education within one of the least literate countries in the world". I would be perfectly happy for DR BAMGBElu to contact myself or my company if he has relevant enquiries to his lease holding, however these continuous letters and emails are causing me distress and I feel intimidated. I am not a racist and these accusatios make uncomfortable. All I want is to conduct between us in a normal manner. I want BambGlu to stop emailing me and sending me letters accusing me of being racist and harassing me." MR ROBERT KINGSTON, SOLICITOR, ACCOUNTANT, AND COMPANY DIRECTOR.

A dyslexic crooked scatter-head white man.

They persecute our people for the dark coat that we neither made nor chose, and cannot change, and they steal the yields of our Christ granted talents, and they impede our ascent from the bottomless crater into which their very, very, greedy racist ancestors threw ours, in the African bush, unprovoked, during several continuous centuries of the greediest economic cannibalism and the evilest racist terrorism the world will ever know — Habakkuk.

He is watching them — Proverbs 15:3.

The nemesis is not extinct, and fact that it tarries isn't proof that it will never come — Habakkuk, Matthew 25: 31–46, and John 5:22.

Then, they won in courts, by hook or by crook, and all the time, but in the war, when the Corporal flipped, the only transparently true Judge looked away, and they lost everything and more than that — Matthew 25: 31 -46, John 5:22.

Some self-educated Africans believe that several years of NAZI HOLOCAUST was a storm in a teacup in comparison to several continuous centuries of European commerce in stolen African children — BLACK HOLOCAUST (the real Holocaust), and they believe that descendants of the victims of NAZI HOLOCAUST are among the principal beneficiaries of several continuous centuries of very, very, greedy, sadistic, inhumane, racist, crude, and cruel commerce in millions of stolen poor black children of defenceless Africans, including the African ancestors of Meghan Markle and her white children — Habakkuk.

Closeted hereditary closeted white supremacist bastards are not the only creation of Almighty God, and they are not immortal, and the universally acknowledged irrefutably superior skin colour that the very, very, fortunate wearer neither made nor chose is not the only wonder of our world.

Skin colour is a great creation of Almighty God, but it is not the greatest.

"Jews are very good with money." President Donald Trump.

Everyone knows that, and the Corporal did too, whose money?

The white man, their President should know a lot about Jews: Bianca and Jared Kushner are Jews.

Judas Iscariot, Ghislaine Maxwell's father, Ján Ludvík Hyman Binyamin Hoch, and Bernard Madoff were Jews.

Gigantic yields of millions of stolen and destroyed children of defenceless poor Africans, including the African ancestors of Meghan Markle and her white children, not feudal agriculture, lured Eastern European Jews to Britain; they changed their names, blended, and latched onto the HUGE STOLEN TRUST FUND.

Latent, but very, very, potent turf war: Racist descendants of aliens with camouflage English names oppress, we, Africans, the descendants of the robbed with the yields of the robbery.

Before Slavery, what?

NEW HEROD: Matthew 2:16:

They lie to their simpler children that they are geniuses, and they kill all those who know that they're brainless racist bastards.

BEDFLORD, ENGLAND: District Judge Paul Robert Ayers, >70, a Mason, and the Senior Vice President of the Association of Her Majesty's District Judges of 3, St Paul's Square, MK 40 1SQ, white man, let me tell you, reasoning and vision are infinite, and the mind that the Nigerian got unsolicited- is finer than the fish and chips legal system that you serve, and it is possible to use cogent facts and irrefutable evidence to irreversibly destroy you and it.

For their legal system to work as designed, they must have supreme knowledge, and they didn't, so when it became apparent that the fellow was intellectual unplayable, He was lynched like Gadhafi and crucified - solely to prevent Him from speaking.

If there is cogent and irrefutable evidence that the white ancestors of one's white mother and father were THIEVES and owners of stolen poor black children of defenceless Africans, including the African ancestors of Meghan Markle and her white children, and if one is a very, very, dishonest racist crook, it's plainly deductible that Freedom Expression is not one's friend.

GDC, 37 Wimpole St, London W1G 8DQ: Jonathan Martin, GDC Executive, Poly-educated white racist rubbish — Not Russell Group Inferior Education — Proverbs 17:16, unrelentingly lied under implied oath — Habakkuk 1:4.

A very, very, crooked racist bastard.

Only his universally acknowledged irrefutably superior skin colour and Almighty God — are truly good — Mark 10:18, and the poly-educated dullard neither made nor chose it, and he will be considerably diminished as a human being without it, and he knows it: WHITE PRIVILEGE.

Mrs Helen Falcon, our Member of the Most Excellent Order of our Empire of Stolen Affluence reminded one of very, very, ugly white Welsh wenches — a white British poet encountered.

"The ordinary women of Wales are generally short and squat, ill-favoured, and nasty." David Mallet (1705–1765).

Then, in the Valleys of Wales, including Nick Griffin's Llanerfyl Powys, there were tens of thousands of white sheep and people, and all the white sheep but not all the people were incestuously conceived, and all the white sheep but not all the people were excessively stupid.

"Wales: The land of my fathers. My fathers can have it."
Dylan Thomas (1914–1953).

Re Meeting 9th March. Mon, 8 Mar 2010 20:20. George
Rothnie georgerothnie@hotmail. comHide. To.
We are scheduled to meet tomorrow evening at my surgery
about 5.30ish. Unfortunately something has cropped up
which necessytates me having to postpone the meeting. I'm
really sorry it's such short notice. I will contact you in the
week to arrange another date.
Once agaim my apologies.
George.

GDC, Dr George Rothnie (Scottish George), Edinburgh
University-Educated Helen Falcon's Deputy Postgraduate
Dean, Oxford, unrelentingly deviated from the truth on
record – Habakkuk 1:4.

Alzheimer's disease is considerably more common than
ordinarily realised.

"What enemy would invade Scotland, where there is
nothing to be got?" Dr Samuel Johnson

Helen Falcon, Member of the Most Excellent Order of
Empire. Our Scatter-head Postgraduate Dean, Oxford
(former).

Our Edinburgh University Educated Prime Minister, our
Scholar from Fife, couldn't spell; then, in our country of the

blind, the partially sighted was our torchbearer, now, our torchbearer worships cows.

"There is in Scotland a diffusion of learning, a certain portion of it widely and thinly spread. A merchant has as much learning as one of their clergies." Dr Samuel Johnson.

ACCURATE SEERS: Very, very, greedy armed racist white bastard Christians accurate foresaw that closeted hereditary racist white privileged dullards will be Postgraduate Tutor, Deputy Postgraduate Dean, and Postgraduate Dean, Oxford, so they embarked on armed robbery and dispossession raids in AFRICA, and wherever the very, very, greedy racist white bastards, and the locals they armed, and drugged (whisky), merciless slaughtered Africans, they dispossessed them, and whenever they robbed Africans, they took possession.

Part of the resultant effects of several centuries of merciless racist, the greediest economic cannibalism, and the evilest racist terrorism the world will ever know, is that white imbecile (predominantly but not exclusively white adults with the basic skills of child), closeted hereditary racist privileged dullards are our Postgraduate Tutor, Deputy Postgraduate Dean, and Postgraduate Dean, Oxford.

BEDFORD, ENGLAND: District Judge Paul Robert Ayers, >70, a Mason, and the Senior Vice President of the Association of Her Majesty's District Judges of 3, St Paul's Square, MK 40 1SQ, apart from creating very, very, cushy salaried jobs for white Solicitors and Barristers (predominantly but not exclusively white) who FAILED in practice, and loads did (quasi-communism), what do closeted hereditary racist white imbeciles (predominantly but not exclusively white adults with the basic skills of a child), need very, very, expensive administration of English Law for?

CHAPTER TWELVE: Letter to the Sovereign, HM (1926 -2022)

"**N**atural selection will not remove ignorance from future generations." Dr Richard Dawkins.

Adults with the basic skills of a foetus will succeed adults with the basic skills of a child, and the former will need only food and shelter.

Our own Nigeria: Shell's docile cash cow since 1956.

Unlike Putin's Russia, there are no oil wells or gas fields in Freemasons' Kempston and where the white mother and father of Bedford's District Judge Paul Robert Ayers, >70, a Mason, and the Senior Vice President of the Association of Her Majesty's District Judges of 3, St Paul's Square, MK 40 1SQ, were born.

Our own Nigerien and Nigerian babies with huge uranium mines, and/or oil wells and gas fields near their huts eat only 1.5/day in our own shit hole Africa, brainless, bellyful closeted hereditary white supremacist bastards whose children might not be able to spell uranium, and whose white ancestors, including the white ancestors of unapologetic white supremacist Sir Winston Churchill (1874–1965) thrive in Great Britain, what is great about that?

Bedford's District Judge Paul Robert Ayers, >70, a Mason, and the Senior Vice President of the Association of Her Majesty's District Judges of 3, St Paul's Square, MK 40 1SQ, let me tell you, reasoning and vision have no finite boundaries.

Act 2:17: The Nigerian is a foetus, what he can see is clearer than dreams, visions, and prophecies, and the mind that he got, unsolicited is finer than the legal system that you serve, and it is possible to use cogent facts and irrefutable evidence to irreversibly destroy you and the legal system you serve.

Bedford's District Judge Paul Robert Ayers, >70, a Mason, and the Senior Vice President of the Association of Her Majesty's District Judges of 3, St Paul's Square, MK 40 1SQ, let me tell you, if you know what I know about you, you will kill me; based on available evidence, the supernatural exists and He is consistently accessible. You cannot go to Him, but He will come to you if you stand where He can come.

"I think I will ask our legal adviser for any advice he may have. My view is that there are six or seven of us here who had the admission down, but we cannot find it in the transcript and there is wordings that imply that there was, but it is not in black and white….." Shiv Pabary, Member of the

Most Excellent Order of our Empire (MBE), the archetypal GDC Committee Chairman, and Justice of Peace (JP).

Our scatter-head imbecile Indian — Uncle Tom.

GDC is part of the evidence that England is dying, and from the head.

Ignoring the grammar of the imbecile Indian (a near perfect imitation of an upper-class English man), he unrelentingly lied under implied oath (on record).

If all the white 33rd Degree Freemasons (predominantly but not exclusively white) at the Provincial Grand Lodge of Northumberland Freemasons, 17 Lansdowne Terrace, Newcastle upon Tyne, NE3 1HP, could disprove that truth that Shiv Pabary, Member of the Most Excellent Order of our Empire (MBE), the archetypal GDC Committee Chairman, and Justice of Peace (JP), LIED when he explicitly stated, "My view is that there are six or seven of us here who had the admission down. …" And if all the white 33rd Degree Freemasons (predominantly but not exclusively white) at the Provincial Grand Lodge of Northumberland Freemasons, 17 Lansdowne Terrace, Newcastle upon Tyne, NE3 1HP, could disprove the truth that Shiv Pabary, Member of the Most Excellent Order of our Empire (MBE), the archetypal GDC Committee Chairman, and Justice of Peace (JP), LIED when he explicitly stated, "…. we cannot find it in the transcript and there is wordings that imply that there was, but it is not in black and white…..", they will confirm the belief of all members of the Anti-Christ Freemasonry Quasi-Religion that their Quasi-Religion is not intellectually flawed, and it is not a confused Satanic Mumbo Jumbo.

It was in the transcript, but closeted racist bastards looked for it in the wrong transcript.

Ian Brack, then, and only there, verdicts were secretly prior agreed inside Freemasons' Temples, and in open Courts, incompetent art incompetently imitated life.

Ian Brack:

Google — Mediocre Great England.

Google — Mediocre GDC.

"….. there is wordings that imply that there was, but it is not in black and white….." Shiv Pabary, Member of the Most Excellent Order of our Empire (MBE), the archetypal GDC Committee Chairman, and Justice of Peace (JP).

A brainless racist Indian bastard.

Our crooked MBE Uncle Tom.

It was not in black and white, but it was written down, so it must have been written in red, gold, black, and green — Reductio ad absurdum.

Then, at Black Market, near The Reverend Henry Carr's (1880–961) Hall, University Lagos, Nigeria, Shit Hole, Africa, where one was a student at the Faculty of Science, and the occupier of Room 237 (1979/1980), and after smoking cheap impure weed, loads of it, and drinking pure, undiluted palm wine, and too much of it, everything, and absolutely everything, including one's fertility tool, and one's urine became red, gold, black, and green.

"How can we sing in a strange land?" Steel Pulse.

Rally round the flag
Rally round the red
Gold black and green

Marcus say sir Marcus say
Red for the blood
That flowed like the river
Marcus say sir Marcus say
Green for the land Africa
Marcus say
Yellow for the gold
That they stole
Marcus say

Black for the people
It was looted from

They took us away captivity captivity
Required from us a song
Right now man say repatriate repatriate

****

According to News, the brother of Shiv Pabary, Member of
the Most Excellent Order of our Empire (MBE), the
archetypal GDC Committee Chairman, and Justice of Peace
(JP), was wonky.

Facts are sacred.

Based on very, very, proximate observations and direct
experiences, Shiv Pabary, Member of the Most Excellent
Order of our Empire (MBE), the archetypal GDC Committee
Chairman, and Justice of Peace (JP), was wonky too,
certainly, intellectually. Their Indian mother and father could
be related (siblings or cousins).

Charles Darwin (1809–1882), married his first cousin and
expectedly, their children, not all, were wonky.

Nigeriens and Nigerians babies with huge uranium mines
and/or oil wells and gas fields near their huts eat oil 1.5/day in

shit hole AFRICA, very, very, bellyful incestuously conceived wonky Indians whose mothers and fathers have seen crude oil, and who might not be able to spell uranium – thrive in Great Britain, what great about that?

Then, in Colonial Africa, the Indian was very happy with any position underneath a white woman if white men placed him above all Africans in the pecking order.

"One witness at a Royal Commission in 1897 said that the ambition of Indians in Trinidad was to buy a cow, then a shop, and say: "We are no Nigg*rs to work in cane fields." Patrick French — 'The World Is What It Is, The Authorised Biography of V.S, Naipaul.

If Ian Brack could disprove the truth that Shiv Pabary, Member of the Most Excellent Order of our Empire (MBE), the archetypal GDC Committee Chairman, and Justice of Peace (JP), was crooked, intellectually incompetent, dishonest, and/or confused, and indiscreetly lied under oath or otherwise deviated from the truth on record, he will confirm the belief of thousands of white dentists (predominantly but not exclusively white), which is that GDC was not intellectually incompetent, mediocre, indiscreetly dishonest, and institutionally racist.

BEDFORD, ENGLAND: District Judge Paul Robert Ayers, >70, a Mason, and the Senior Vice President of the Association of Her Majesty's District Judges of 3, St Paul's

Square, MK 40 1SQ, facts are sacred, and they cannot be overstated. Our own MONEY, Nigeria (oil/gas) is by far more relevant to the economic survival of all your own white children, your white spouse, your white mother, and your white father than LUTON. Based on cogent, irrefutable, and available evidence, the white ancestors of your white mother and father were THIEVES and owners of stolen poor black children of defenceless Africans, including the black African ancestors of the white great grandchildren of Prince Phillip (1921–2021).

Philippians 1:21: Was Phillip a 33rd Degree Freemason, Scottish Rite?

CHAPTER THIRTEEN: Dr Ngozi Ekweremadu, a
Nigerian whistleblower.

"They may not have been well written from a grammatical
point of view .." Geraint Evans, our Postgraduate Tutor,
Oxford

"The best opportunity of developing academically and
emotional." Bedford's District Judge Paul Robert Ayers, >70,
a Mason, and the Senior Vice President of the Association of
Her Majesty's District Judges of 3, St Paul's Square, MK 40
1SQ, proof-read and approved Judgement.

A functional semi-illiterate closeted hereditary genetic alien
impersonates the aboriginal Briton.

No Brain.

Poor in natural resources. Unlike Putin's Russia, there are no
oil wells or gas fields in LUTON and where his own white
mother and father were born.

Several continuous centuries of stealing and slavery preceded
the GIGANTIC stolen trust fund.

WHITE PRIVILEGE: Only his universally acknowledged irrefutably superior skin colour and Almighty God are truly good – Mark 10:18, and he neither made nor chose it, and he will be considerably diminished as a human being without it, and he knows it.

Nigerians and Nigeriens children with huge uranium mines and/or oil wells and gas fields near their huts eat only 1.5/day in our own shit hole Africa, bellyful brainless functional semi-illiterate racist white bastards whose white mothers and fathers have never seen uranium or crude oil, and whose mentally gentler children might not be able to spell uranium, and whose white ancestors were fed like battery hens with yields of stolen poor black children of defenceless Africans, including the black African ancestors of Meghan Markle and her white children — thrive in great Britain, what's great about unashamed mediocrity and confusion?

OYINBO OMO OLE: OYINBO OMO ALE:

They are functional semi-illiterates crooked hereditary closeted white supremacist bastards, unlike Putin's Russia, there are no oil wells or gas fields where their white mothers and fathers were born, and they are relatively rich, and they dishonestly implied that they didn't know that the white ancestors of their white mothers and fathers were THIEVES and owners of stolen children of defenceless Africans, including the black African ancestors of the great grandchildren of the Sovereign — Habakkuk

"It was our arms in the river of Cameroon, put into the hands of the trader, that furnished him with the means of pushing his trade; and I have no more doubt that they are British arms, put into the hands of Africans, which promote universal war and desolation that I can doubt their having done so in that individual instance. I have shown how great is the enormity of this evil, even on the supposition that we take only convicts and prisoners of war. But take the subject in another way, and how does it stand? Think of 80,000 persons carried out of their native country by, we know not what means! For crimes imputed! For light or inconsiderable faults! For debts perhaps! For the crime of witchcraft! Or a thousand other weak or scandalous pretexts! Reflect on 80,000 persons annually taken off! There is something in the horror of it that surpasses all bounds of imagination." — Prime Minister William Pitt the Younger

Properly rehearsed ultra-righteousness and deceptively schooled civilised decorum were preceded by several continuous centuries of merciless racist evil — Habakkuk.

"England is like a prostitute who, having sold her body all her life, decides to quit her business, and then tells everybody she wants to be chaste and protect her flesh as if it were jade." He Manzi

A brainless poly-educated functional semi-illiterate closeted hereditary white supremacist bastard rides a tiger, and deluded, he thinks he is it, dismounted, he will instantly revert to NOTHING.

Google: Imagbon 1892: If he were to do a walk about in our tribe (Ijebu), in the African bush, the closeted hereditary white supremacist bastard might be lynched like Gadhafi, and what can their Indian do about it.

A brainless poly-educated functional semi-illiterate closeted hereditary white supremacist bastard sat on a very, very, highchair that the people of Bedford couldn't and didn't buy — in our Cathedral Court that was preceded by SLAVERY, future flats.

29, Goldington Road is a block of flats.

BEDFORD, ENGLAND: District Judge, which part of our County Court, 3, St Paul's Square, MK 40 1SQ, wasn't stolen, or which part of it is the yield of the very, very, High IQs of your own white mother and father, or which part of it preceded SLAVERY: The building or its chattels? OYINBO ODE.

The only evidence of his very, very, High IQ is the stolen affluence that his thoroughly wretched white ancestors crossed the English Channels, without luggage or decent shoes, to latch onto - Habakkuk.

"I emphasis the point." Bedford's District Judge Paul Robert Ayers, >70, a Mason, and the Senior Vice President of the Association of Her Majesty's District Judges of 3, St Paul's Square, MK 40 1SQ,

A brainless racist white bastard.

Mistakes should not occur in properly proofed and approved Judgement by properly educated Senior Judges in our own NIGERIA.

In our own NIGERIA, properly proofed and approved Judgements by properly educated Senior Judges should pass through at least four separate filters: The transcript writers, the proof-readers, the Court Clerks, and the Judge.

In an open dialogue with Justice Ruth Bader Ginsburg (1933 – 2020), Lady Hale lamented funding.

My Lady, what's the value of several layers of unashamed mediocrity and confusion?

If all the Jews, and all members of the Freemasonry Fraternity, in the world could disprove the truth that ILFORD, ESSEX: Mr Robert Kingston, Solicitor, Accountant, and Director Dobern Property Limited, albeit England's Class, unrelentingly deviated from the truth under implied oath (on record), and if they could disprove the truth that Bedford's District Judge Paul Robert Ayers, >70, a Mason, and the Senior Vice President of the Association of Her Majesty's District Judges unrelentingly deviated from the truth under oath (approved Judgement), and if they could disprove that BEDFORD, ENGLAND: GDC, Freemason, Brother Richard William Hill (NHS postgraduate graduate tutor) fabricated

reports and unrelentingly lied under oath — Habakkuk 1:4,
and if they could disprove the truth that BEDFORD,
ENGLAND: GDC, Sue Gregory, Officer of the Most
Excellent Order of our Empire (OBE), unrelentingly lied
under implied oath, and if they could disprove the truth that
OXFORD, ENGLAND: GDC, Bristol University Educated
Mrs Helen Falcon, Member of the Most Excellent Order of
our Empire, former Member of the GDC Committee,
Rotarian (auxiliary Freemason), former Postgraduate Dean,
Oxford, and the only spouse of Mr Falcon, unrelentingly lied
under implied oath (on record), and if they could disprove
that OXFORD, ENGLAND: GDC, Stephanie Twidale,
British Soldier, Territorial Defence (TD), unrelentingly lied
under oath, and if they could disprove the truth that
homunculus man, Anthony Kravitz, Officer of the Most
Excellent Order of our Empire knew or ought to know that
Stephanie Twidale (TD) unrelentingly lied under oath, and if
they could disprove that Geraint Evans, our Welsh
Postgraduate Tutor, Oxford, unrelentingly lied under implied
oath, and if they , could disprove the truth that OXFORD,
ENGLAND: GDC/MPS, Stephen Henderson, LLM, BDS,
Head at MDDUS — did not deviate from the truth on record,
and if they could disprove the truth that NORTHAMPTON,
ENGLAND: GDC, Ms Rachael Bishop, Senior NHS Nurse,
unrelentingly lied under oath, and if they could disprove the
truth that SCOTLAND, ENGLAND: GDC, Kevin Atkinson
(Scottish Kev), Postgraduate Tutor, Oxford, unrelentingly lied
under oath, and if they could disprove the truth that
SCOTLAND, ENGLAND: GDC, George Rothnie (Scottish
George), our Deputy Postgraduate Dean, Oxford,
unrelentingly deviated from the truth on record, and

LONDON, ENGLAND: GDC, Poly-educated Jonathan Martin (not Russell Group Inferior Education — Proverbs 17:16) unrelentingly lied on record, and if they could disprove the truth that Shiv Pabary, Member of the Most Excellent of our Empire (MBE), the archetypal GDC Committee Chairman, and Justice of Peace (JP), Homunculus man, Anthony Kravitz, Officer of the Most Excellent Order of our Empire (OBE), David Swinstead, the archetypal GDC Committee Legal Adviser, Mr Jaques Lee, Ms Mary Harley, David Morris, Nicholas Peacock, Andrew Hurst, now, a Circuit Judge, albeit England's Class, did not know and/or ought not to know that GDC, Richard William Hill fabricated reports and unrelentingly lied under oath, GDC, Ms Rachael Bishop, Senior NHS Nurse, unrelentingly lied under oath, GDC, Kevin Atkinson (Scottish Kev), Postgraduate Tutor, Oxford, unrelentingly lied under oath, GDC, British Soldier, Stephanie Twidale (TD), unrelentingly lied under oath, they will confirm the belief of billions of people in our world, which is that Antichrist Freemasonry Quasi-Religion (Mediocre Mafia, New Pharisees, New Good Samaritans, Defenders of Faiths, including all the exotic faiths and religions associated with the 15 Holy Books in the House of Commons, and Dissenters of the Faith — John 14:6), Antichrist Islam, Antichrist Judaism, and other motley assemblies of exotic religions and faiths under the common umbrella of the Governor of the Church of England and the Defender of the Faith — John 14:6, are not intellectually flawed Satanic Mumbo Jumbo, and it will also confirm that reasoning and vision have finite boundaries, and if reasoning and vision have finite boundaries, the fellow must have lied, in the Council, before Jews and Romans, when He disclosed pictures His unbounded mind painted, and He must have also lied when, with arrogant audacity, he stated that He was exceptional — John 14:6. "The first quality that is needed is audacity." Churchill. If the fellow to the truth, in the Council, before Romans and Jews, we are all FORKED, all of us, no one is good — Psalm 53, as His Knights attacks all Queens and Kings simultaneously, and only the Queens could move, and everything that is aligned with the exceptionalism of the fellow is travelling in the wrong direction, and heading straight for the rocks.

OYINBO OMO OLE: OYINBO OMO ALE.

They hate us, and more than their racist ancestors hated ours. The only part of our own AFRICA they truly love is our own money (diverse natural resources), absolutely everything else is deceit.

Then, very, very, greedy racist white bastards carried and sold millions of stolen poor black children of defenceless Africans, including the black African ancestors of Meghan Markle's white children, now, they steal our own natural resources from our own shit hole African.

 Substitution is fraudulent emancipation.

"Moderation is a virtue only among those who are thought to have alternatives." Henry Kissinger.

CHAPTER FOURTEEN: Letter to the Sovereign, HM (1926 – 2022).

Politicians come and go, but they never leave, and they do vulgar Pharisees' charitable works with stolen money.

How many charitable works did BUILDERS do before SLAVERY?

Hereditary white supremacist thugs want superiority, their brainless and baseless birth right, they can have it, but based on MERIT, or Christ granted talent, what's wrong with that?

https://www.youtube.com/watch?v=BlpH4hG7m1A

BEDFORD, ENGLAND: GDC, Freemason, Brother, Richard William Hill, (NHS) fabricated reports and unrelentingly lied under oath – Habakkuk 1:4.

A very, very, dishonest white man.

A crooked closeted hereditary white supremacist Freemason. Closeted hereditary white supremacist bastards are very, very, highly civilised and super-enlightened, and they adhere strictly to rule of their law, and they do everything legally, including racial hatred fraud, and they legally fabricate reports and unrelentingly tell lies under oath, and in doing so ignorant racist bastards adhere strictly to Civil Procedure Rules, Statute, and Precedent.

1976 – 2022: A brainless incontrovertibly functional semi-illiterate opportunist hereditary racist white bastard. A mere former debt-collector Solicitor in NORWICH (5th Rate Partner). Having FAILED in practice, loads of white Solicitors and Barristers did (predominantly but not exclusively white), he parked his liability at the public till, and sold unashamed mediocrity and confusion to the undiscerning, and to the discerning who couldn't go elsewhere.

Some people FAILED in practice because they were very, very, sloppy, and their discerning clients went elsewhere, and they parked their liability at the public till where those who look down on their mediocre talent and continuing sloppiness must buy the services they render.

The Senior Judge, albeit England's Class, must have known who his white kindred Mrs Lisa Thomas was before constructively coaching his white kindred to call their white kindred, Mrs Lisa Thomas.

******

DISTRICT JUDGE AYERS: Well, you'd better, I think, call your client or Mrs. Thomas to give evidence, to deal with the issues that are outstanding.

MR. PURKIS: Certainly, sir. May I call Mrs. Thomas?

Mrs. L. Thomas
Examined by Mr. Purkis.

Q. Mrs. Thomas, you have a bundle in front of you, and I believe that if you turn to page 141, you'll see a document there that says at the top, 'Witness statement of Lisa Thomas.' Is that your witness statement?

A. That's correct.

Q. If we turn to paragraph 8 there, it says, 'In the circumstances, I respectfully ask the court to enter judgment for the amount claimed of £410.66,' then it says, 'which comprises of the court fee for issuing the claim, totalling £95, and solicitors fees on issuing of £80.' Can I confirm that those fees of £95 and £80 aren't in fact included in that £410.66?

A. No, there is an error.

DISTRICT JUDGE AYERS: Right. Before we go any further, Mr. Purkis, we'd better have your client telling me who she is.

******

Then, in some parts of the world, Freemasons oversaw the administration of the law, and verdicts were prior agreed in Freemasons Temples, and in open courts, incompetent art incompetently imitated life.

BEDFORD, ENGLAND: GDC, Sue Gregory, Officer of the Most Excellent Order of our Empire (OBE), unrelentingly lied under implied oath – Habakkuk 1:4.

A very, very, dishonest white woman.

A racist crooked Officer of the Most Excellent Order of our Empire of Stolen Affluence.

Our Empire did not evolve from NOTHING, then, almost everything was actively and deliberately stolen with guns.

"Affluence is not a birth right." David Cameron (a former premier)

Why did white Senior Judge, albeit England's Class, wait until his white kindred stated that there was an error before asking his white kindred ask his white kindred to tell him who she was, if the sole purpose of breaking the chain of disclosure was not to prevent the semi-illiterate white woman to expatiate on the ERROR.

They are THIEVES, and they are the direct descendants of THIEVES and owners of stolen poor black children of defenceless Africans.

They hate us, and we know. They love only our money, Africa's diverse natural resources, and absolutely everything else is intelligently designed deceit.

Then, armed greedy racist white bastards and those they armed used guns to steal for the benefit of their own white kindred, now, they use incompetent racist lies to steal for the benefit of their own white kindred.

Their law is equal for blacks and whites, but the administration of their law is not, and the administration of their law is meat, and it is a very, very, potent weapon of RACE WAR.

Then, and only there, Freemasons oversaw the administration of their law, and there was absolutely NOTHING they couldn't do under their bendable and breakable law.

BEDFORD, ENGLAND: GDC, Freemason, Brother, Richard William Hill (NHS Postgraduate Tutor, Bedfordshire), unrelentingly lied under oath – Habakkuk 1:4.

A very, very, dishonest white man.

A crooked racist descendant of industrial-scale professional thieves and owners of stolen poor black children of defenceless Africans, including the black African children of Meghan Markle and her white children – Habakkuk.

CHAPTER FIFTEEN: Dr Ngozi Ekweremadu, a Nigerian whistleblower

When the real freedom of expression, (President Thomas Jefferson's level of the First Amendment), becomes a basic right, under law - very, very, charitable Antichrist Freemasonry Quasi-Religion (Mediocre Mafia, New Pharisees, New Good Samaritans, Defenders of Faiths, including all the exotic faiths and religions associated with the 15 Holy Books in the House of Commons, and Dissenters of the Faith – John 14:6) will be uncovered and destroyed.

Vulgar Pharisees' charitable works in exchange for what? Theirs is not a good deal – Matthew 4:9.

How many charitable works did Freemasons do before SLAVERY?

Before Freemasons' RACIAL HATRED guarded by incompetent mendacity unravels, it is always a conspiracy theory, and when it does, it instantly mutates to a mistake.

What exactly is the point of Civil Procedure Rules (CPR), Statute, and Precedent, in an indiscreetly institutionally racist legal system that allows white people, only white people, to fabricate reports and tell incompetent racist lies under oath?

Then, they (Freemasons) were like RATS, and like rats they loved to act without being seen, and like rats , they were excessively stupid, as they defecated everywhere leaving tell-tale scars.

Once you can see them, and they know you can, especially if you are a mere Negur from shit hole Africa, you have inadvertently reached the end of your life, as the loose end must be tied by hook or by crook, and their preferred method of killing was hands-off; they killed foreigners through economic strangulation, and their people were everywhere, and controlled almost everything.

Google: Dr Anand Kamath, Dentist.

Google: Dr Richard Bamgboye, GP.

"Many Scots masters were considered among the most brutal, with life expectancy on their plantations averaging a mere four years. We worked them to death then simply imported more to keep the sugar and thus the money flowing. Unlike centuries of grief and murder, an apology cost nothing. So, what does Scotland have to say?" Herald Scotland: Ian Bell, Columnist, Sunday 28 April 2013

IGNORANT RACIST FOOLS: Very, very, highly civilised, super-enlightened, and ultra-righteous descendants of extremely nasty THIEVES and owners of stolen poor black children of defenceless poor people, including the black African ancestors of Meghan Markle and her white children.

Based on cogent, irrefutable, and available evidence, properly rehearsed ultra-righteousness, and deceptively schooled civilised decorum were preceded by several continuous centuries of merciless racist evil: The greediest economic cannibalism and the evilest racist terrorism the world will ever know – Habakkuk.

"It was our arms in the river of Cameroon, put into the hands of the trader, that furnished him with the means of pushing his trade; and I have no more doubt that they are British arms, put into the hands of Africans, which promote universal war and desolation that I can doubt their having done so in that individual instance. I have shown how great is the enormity of this evil, even on the supposition that we take only convicts and prisoners of war. But take the subject in another way, and how does it stand? Think of 80,000 persons carried out of their native country by, we know not what means! For crimes imputed! For light or inconsiderable faults! For debts perhaps! For the crime of witchcraft! Or a thousand other weak or scandalous pretexts! Reflect on 80,000 persons annually taken off! There is something in the horror of it that surpasses all bounds of imagination." – Prime Minister William Pitt the Younger.

"I know of no evil that has ever existed, nor can imagine any evil to exist, worse than the tearing of eighty thousand persons annually from their native land, by a combination of the most civilised nations inhabiting the most enlightened part of the globe, but more especially under the sanction of the laws of that Nation which calls herself the most free and the most happy of them all." Prime Minister William Pitt the Younger

Those who shipped millions of guns to AFRICA (about 200,000 guns manufactured in Birmingham were shipped to shit hole Africa annually) during several continuous centuries of merciless RACIST EVIL: The greediest economic cannibalism and the evilest racist terrorism the world will ever know (Habakkuk) – were very, very, bellyful, most free, and most happy, but they were neither civilised nor enlightened, and they were not CHRISTIANS.

Armed racist bastards, very, very, highly civilised, and super-enlightened European Christians were greedier than the grave, and like death, they were never satisfied – Habakkuk 2:5.

They are no longer here, but it will be very, very, naïve not to expect their genes of merciless racial hatred, sadism, and savagery to continue to flow through the veins of their direct descendants who remain here.

Equitable and just reparation pend, and several centuries of unpaid interest accrue.

OYINBO OMO OLE: OYINBO OMO ALE.

******

Q. If we turn to paragraph 8 there, it says, 'In the circumstances, I respectfully ask the court to enter judgment for the amount claimed of £410.66,' then it says, 'which comprises of the court fee for issuing the claim, totalling £95, and solicitors fees on issuing of £80.' Can I confirm that those fees of £95 and £80 aren't in fact included in that £410.66?

A. No, there is an error.

DISTRICT JUDGE AYERS: Right. Before we go any further, Mr. Purkis, we'd better have your client telling me who she is.

MR. PURKIS: Very well, sir. Could you give your full name to the court?

A. My name is Mrs. Lisa Jane Thomas, I'm property manager for Residential Block Management Services, and our clients are Dobern Properties.

Q. And how long have you been managing this particular block?

A. From around December 2010 when we was instructed by the previous agents. They were the administrators.

MR. BAMGBELU: Do you have proof of that?

******

Then, everyone in Great Britain was white, and nearly all white Judges were Freemasons, and some of them were thicker than a gross of planks.

Your Majesty in Heaven, near our Father in Heaven, in another era, and now, English law was, and remains, transparently equal for all your subjects, but then, and now, the administration of English was not, and remains, unequal, for blacks and whites.

"All sections of UK society are institutionally racist." Sir Bernard Hogan-Howe, KBE, a former Metropolitan Police Chief.

Your Majesty, the Antichrist closeted white supremacist Freemasonry Religion (Mediocre Mafia, New Pharisees, New Good Samaritans, Defenders of Faiths, including all the faiths and religions associated with the 15 Holy Books in the House of Commons, and Dissenters of the Faith – John 14:6), the Police Force, and the Judiciary are parts of UK society.

"Racism is rife throughout most organisations across Britain." The Mayor of London

"Meghan Markle was the victim of explicit and obnoxious RACIAL HATRED." John Bercow, a former speaker.

BEDFORD, ENGLAND: District Judge Paul Robert Ayers, >70, a Mason, and the Senior Vice President of the Association of Her Majesty's District Judges of 3, St Paul's Square, MK 40 1SQ, based on proximate observations and direct experiences, you are worthy only because you're white and England is very rich. It is absolutely impossible for your talent and yields of the land on which your white father and mother were born. The yield of the land and the talents of your white ancestors of your white mother and father did not sustain their standard of living. Based on available evidence, the white ancestors of your white mother and father were industrial-scale PROFESSIONAL THIEVES, extremely nasty racist murderers, armed robbers, armed land grabbers, and owners of stolen poor black children of defenceless Africans, including the West African ancestors of the white great grandchildren of Prince Phillip (1921 – 2021).

"Jesus is the Bedrock of my faith." HM (1926 – 2022).

Philippian 1:21. Was Phillip a 33rd Degree Freemason – Scottish Rite?

Ignorant closeted hereditary white supremacist bastards wear vulgar Pharisees' charitable works as cloaks of deceit, and they use very, very, expensive colourful shiny aprons, with vulgarly ostentatious embroideries to decorate the temples of their powerless and useless fertility tools, and they brainlessly and baselessly awarded themselves the supreme knowledge, and they tell lies all the time, but the lie that they don't lie – Psalm 144.

"Lies are told all the time." Sir Michael Havers (1923 – 1992), our Attorney General, 1980.

Your Majesty, if you were the Defender of the Faith, and if
'the Faith' are bywords of John 14:6, it was plainly
deductible that Christ was the cornerstone of your Faith.
So, your explicit statement seemed to be principally aimed
at the BUILDERS: Integrity, friendship, Respect, and
Charity.

The stone that the builders rejected is now the cornerstone
– Psalm 118:22, Luke 20:17.

Your Majesty in Heaven, near our Father in Heaven, based
on several decades of very, very, proximate observations
and direct experiences, their people are everywhere, and
deluded closeted hereditary white supremacist bastards are
omnipresent Antichrist demigods, and they control almost
everything in Great Britain - FREEMASONS.

Your Majesty in Heaven, near our Father in Heaven, based
on cogent, irrefutable, and available evidence, when closeted
hereditary white supremacist bastards committed racist
crimes against your black subjects, white Freemason Judges
who oversaw the administration of the law – criminally
buried racial hatred – CONFLICT OF INTEREST.

Your Majesty in Heaven, near our Father in Heaven, then
and now, Charitable Freemasons are, essentially, closeted
hereditary white supremacist thugs – who baselessly and
brainlessly awarded themselves the supreme knowledge, and
who delude themselves that they know all, and see all, albeit

with prior predilection and prejudice tainted 20/20, and the closeted hereditary white supremacist thugs are very, very, very, active in the administration of English Law.

BEDFORD, ENGLAND: Your Majesty, based on cogent, irrefutable, available evidence, GDC, Freemason, Brother, Richard William Hill, NHS Postgraduate Tutor, fabricated reports and unrelentingly lied under oath – Habakkuk 1:4.

A very, very, dishonest white man.

A very, very, crooked, and racist NHS Postgraduate Tutor of our Empire of Stolen Affluence – Habakkuk.

Facts are sacred, and they cannot be overstated.

Your Majesty in Heaven, near our Father in Heaven, as a permanent residence of Heaven, you should have access to all TRUTHS.

Your Majesty in Heaven, near our Father in Heaven, then and now, Charitable Antichrist Freemasons (Mediocre Mafia, New Pharisees, New Good Samaritans, Defenders of Faiths, including all the Faiths associated with the 15 Holy Books in the House of Commons, and Dissenters of the Faith – John 14:6) - are showing your African former subjects – pepper, and we do not like pepper soup.

Your Majesty in Heaven, near our Father in Heaven, if all the members of the Antichrist hereditary white supremacist Freemasonry Quasi-Religion (Mediocre Mafia, New Pharisees, New Good Samaritans, Defenders of Faiths, including all the religions and faiths associated with the 15 Holy Books in the House of Commons, and Dissenters of the Faith – John 14:6), and including all the Freemason Judges in Bedfordshire, could disprove the truth that GDC, Freemason, Brother, Richard William Hill, NHS Postgraduate Tutor, fabricated reports and unrelentingly lied under oath – Habakkuk 1:4, they will confirm the belief of scores of millions of Britons, which is that very, very, very, charitable Antichrist Freemasonry Quasi-Religion (Mediocre Mafia, New Pharisees, New Good Samaritans, Defenders of faiths, including the motley assemblies of exotic faiths and religions – associated with the 15 Holy Books in the House of commons, and Dissenters of the Faith – John 14:6), Antichrist Islam, Antichrist Judaism, and all other Great Religions and Faiths, including the religion of our Premier, our torchbearer, which relates to the worship of cows, are not intellectually flawed SATANIC MUMBO JUMBO, and it will confirm that reasoning and vision have finite boundaries, and if reasoning and vision have finite boundaries, our own Messiah must have lied, in the Council, before Jews and Romans, when He, purportedly disclosed pictures His unbounded mind painted, and the fellow must have also lied when He audaciously stated that He was exceptional – John 14:6.

"The first quality that is needed is audacity." Sir Winston Churchill

If the bedrock of HM's (1926 – 2022) Faith – told Jews and Romans the truth, in the Council, we are all FORKED, and BIG TIME, as the Knights of the supernatural fellow with infinite reasoning and vision attack Kings and Queens simultaneously, and only Queens can escape the attack, so CHECKMATE, and everything that is not aligned to the notion of unbounded reasoning and vision is travelling in the wrong direction, and heading straight for very, very, hard rocks.

Facts are Holy, and they cannot be overstated.

CHAPTER SIXTEEN: Letter to the Sovereign, HM (1926 – 2022)

"It does no harm to throw the occasional man overboard, but it does not do much good if you are steering full speed ahead for the rocks." Sir Ian Gilmour

WHITE PRIVILEGE: Unlike President Joe Biden and President Zelensky, President Putin does not want Ukrainians to be part of our very, very, highly civilised, and super enlightened Free World, where white people, including white Freemasons, and only white people, are allowed to fabricate reports and unrelentingly tell incompetent racist lies, including under oath (Negrophobic Perjury guides and guards Persecutory Negrophobia), so he converted Bakhmut of our eyes to Bakhmut of our hearts, as bricks were ruthlessly converted to rubble.

Your Majesty, in 1892, armed Britons, and inferior cultured aliens they armed, converted our Ijebu Ode, our city of our eyes to the Ijebu Ode of our hearts. Then clay huts were converted to sand. Then, armed racist bastards evicted the Awujale (our King) from his palace, and burnt all the ancient gods, and dry wood carving burnt very well, and they converted Afin Awujale (our King's Palace) to their Garrison, and in 1893 scores of Ijebu Ode girls, including children, gave birth to Mulattos.

Then, there was Sex-Machine in the African Bush.

There is NOTHING new under the sun.

Google: Imagbon 1892

Your Majesty in Heaven, near our Father in Heaven, it is deductible that the white ancestors of the white mother and father of GDC, Freemason, Brother, Richard William Hill, NHS Postgraduate Tutor, were accurate seers, and they foresaw that their white descendant will be scatter-head and crooked, so they embarked on armed robbery and dispossession raids in AFRICA, and whenever they, and those they armed, used guns to mercilessly slaughter AFRICANS carrying sticks and stones, they dispossessed, and wherever sadistic greedy racist bastards robbed AFRICANS of their possessions, they took possessions - Habakkuk

Then, and only there,]everyone was white, and most of the Judges were Masons, and the nomination and constructive appointment of white Mason Judges, by dementing or demented white Freemason Lords, wasn't based on colour-blind and measurable objectivity, so an imbecile could become a Judge in Great Britain.

"It is incumbent upon the court and all those professionals involved to conclude court proceedings as quickly as possible. This hopefully ensures that a child has stability, love and affection and the parents working together to ensure that he has the best opportunity of developing academically and emotional." Bedford's District Judge Paul Robert Ayers, > 70, a Mason, and the Senior Vice President of the Association of Her Majesty's District Judges, of 3, St Paul's Square, MK 40 1SQ – Proofed and Approved Judgement.

OYINBO ODE. OYINBO OLODO.

A brainless racist white bastard.

An ultra-righteous descendant of THIEVES and owners of stolen poor black children of defenceless Africans, including the African ancestors of Meghan Markle and her white children – Habakkuk.

"I don't want to talk grammar. I want to talk like a lady." George Bernard Shaw (1856 – 1950).

Our imbecile closeted hereditary white supremacist Freemason District Judge of our Empire of Stolen Affluence - Habakkuk.

An ignorant semi-literate poly-educated former debt-collector Solicitor in Norwich (a former 5th Rate Partner in Norwich), an unashamedly functional semi-illiterate fruit picker impersonates a Senior District Judge – Habakkuk 1:4.

Only his superior skin colour is good, and he neither made nor chose it, and he will be considerably diminished as a human being without it, and he knows it.

Facts are Holy, and they cannot be overstated.

Alzheimer's disease is colour-blind, and it is considerably more common than ordinarily realised.

Does their 80-year-old President suffer from incipient Alzheimer's disease?

Then, some scatter-head closeted white supremacist Mason Judges suffered from Alzheimer' disease or latent progressive dementia.

Bedford's District Judge Paul Robert Ayers, > 70, a Mason, and the Senior Vice President of the Association of Her Majesty's District Judges, of 3, St Paul's Square, MK 40 1SQ, approved and immortalised what his own functional semi-literate white mother and father spoke (deductible), the type of stories his own semi-literate white father used to tell when he returned from Queen Victoria, at odd hours, and thoroughly stoned, and which his poly-educated white supervisors and superiors in Luton authorised.

HHJ Perusko studied law at Poly (Not Russell Group Inferior Education — Proverbs 17:16).

"To survive, you must tell stories …... I believe that what we become depends on what our fathers teach us at odd moments, when they aren't trying to teach us. We are formed by little scraps of wisdom." Umberto Eco.

A corrupt and indiscreetly racist legal system that is overseen by closeted white supremacist Freemason Judges — Habakkuk 1:4.

Putin does not want Ukrainian to be part of our Free World where Freedom of Expression is the cornerstone of our democracy and where a crooked and/or confused white woman could become an Officer of the Most Excellent Order of our Empire, so he converted Mariupol from bricks to rubble.

If a crooked and/or confused white woman is an Officer of the Most Excellent Order of our Empire, it is plainly deductible that Freedom of Expression is not her friend.

Part of the resultant effects of several centuries of stealing and slavery is that a crooked and/or confused white woman is an Officer of the Most Excellent Order of our Empire.

A closeted racist white bastard sat on a very, very, hardwood highchair that the people of Bedford couldn't and didn't buy - in a Cathedral Court that was preceded by Slavery, future flats.

29, Goldington Road is a block of flats, and it was preceded by SLAVERY.

Prior to SLAVERY, there weren't very, very, many proper houses in BEDFORD.

White Eastern European Christians and Jews are mercilessly slaughtering each other because Putin does not want Ukrainians to be part of our institutionally racist Free World where white people, only white people are allowed to criminally fabricate reports and tell incompetent lies under oath, albeit with due regard to precedent, statute, and civil procedure rules (CPR).

Crass!

GDC, 37 Wimpole St, London W1G 8DQ: Poly-educated Jonathan Martin, unrelentingly lied under oath (on record) — Habakkuk.

White skin concealed a dark black brain.

A very, very dishonest poly-educated white man: Not Russell Group Inferior Education – Proverbs 17:16.

A Racist White Crook.

Jonathan Martin, GDC Executive, which part of 37 Wimpole St, London W1G 8DQ preceded SLAVERY, or which part of it is the yield of the Higher IQs of your own white mother: The building or its chattels?

Jonathan Martin, GDC Executive, 37 Wimpole St, London W1G 8DQ, unlike Putin's Russia, there are no oil wells or gas fields in Birmingham and where your own white mother and father were born. An ignorant descendant of THIEVES and owners of stolen children of defenceless Africans, including the African ancestors of Meghan Markle and her white children – Habakkuk.

Jonathan Martin, GDC Executive, 37 Wimpole St, London W1G 8DQ, if there is irrefutable evidence that the white ancestors of one's white mother and father were THIEVES and owners of stolen poor black children of defenceless Africans, including the African ancestors of Meghan Markle and her white children,, it will be very, very, very, naïve not to expect RACIAL HATRED (Persecutory Negrophobia) guided and guarded by criminalised incompetent mendacity (Negrophobic Perjury), to be part of one's genetic inheritances, and it should be plainly deductible that Freedom of Expression is not one's friend – Habakkuk.

Based on available evidence, it's not the truth that UKRAINE is the only corrupt country in Europe.

Google: The White Judge Lied.

No one is good, not one — Psalm 53.

Based on several decades of very proximate observations and direct experiences, very, very, charitable Freemasons are more intolerant to the exceptionalism of Christ (John 14:6) than lunatic Jihadists.

Your Majesty in Heaven, near our Father in Heaven, we don't need to report racist white bastards to closeted white supremacist Freemason Judges, as demons can't cast out demons — Matthew 12:27,

Your Majesty in Heaven, near our Father in Heaven, we are consoled by the fact that our racist oppressor aren't immortal, so racist oppression is finite, and there is a transparently just Judge who sees all and knows all, and he will Judge all, including crooked closeted hereditary white supremacist Freemason Judges — John 5:22, Matthew 25:31–46, and Proverbs 15:3.

Your Majesty in Heaven, near our Father in Heaven, based on proximate observations and direct experiences, very, very, charitable Freemasons are RACISTS, intellectually incompetent, envious, shallow, and extremely dangerous – Habakkuk 1:4.

Vindictive Racist White Bastards, New Herod, Matthew 2:16: Racist white bastards see molecules and they destroy all self-educated Africans who see atoms.

Your Majesty in Heaven, near our Father in Heaven, He was lynched like Gadhafi and crucified only because He spoke; He disclosed pictures His unbounded mind painted. He was not punished for speaking, He was lynched like Gadhafi and crucified – solely to prevent Him from speaking. Shallow ignorant bastards (Jews and Romans) saw molecules, and He saw quarks, and since they had brainlessly and baselessly awarded themselves supreme knowledge, and they had unbounded and unaccountable power, they criminally destroyed all those who disagreed with them, albeit 'legally'.

Christianity, European Civilisation, and European Laws – based on Christianity preceded several continuous centuries of barbarously racist, sadistic, crude, and cruel traffic in millions of stolen poor black children of defenceless Africans, including the African ancestors of Meghan Markle's white children – Habakkuk.

An opportunist racist descendant of undocumented refugees from Eastern Europe, with arbitrarily acquired camouflage English names, galivants about the place like Royalty. Like his mentally gentler children, the white imbeciles (predominantly but not exclusively white adults with the basic skills of a child) who sat before him, in our Cathedral Court that was preceded by Slavery, didn't know that his nomination, and constructive appointment, by dementing or demented white Lords, was not based on progressive, colour-blind, and measurable objectivity, and they did not know that the last time the opportunist white supremacist bastard passed through the filter of non-chromatic objectivity was when he studied 5th rate law at poly, and it showed.

Then, Alzheimer's disease was not uncommon among Lords.

Then, Alzheimer's disease was considerably more common than ordinarily realised, and it was not compatible with the competent administration of English Law.

The competent administration of English Law is an inviolable basic right.

"Should 500 men, ordinary men, chosen accidentally from among the unemployed, override the judgement — the deliberate judgement — of millions of people who are engaged in the industry which makes the wealth of the country?" David Lloyd George (1863 – 1945).

"This man I thought had been a Lord of wits, but I find he is only a wit among Lords." Dr Samuel Johnson.

Bedford, England: District Judge Paul Robert Ayers, > 70, a Mason, and the Senior Vice President of the Senior Vice President of the Association of Her Majesty's District Judges, of 3, St Paul's Square, MK40 1SQ, based on available evidence, English Law is equal for blacks and whites, but its administration is not, and it is the worst form of Apartheidism. Only stupid Africans expect closeted white supremacist Freemason Judges to measure blacks with the same yardstick they use to measure whites, and only stupider Africans expect demons to cast out demons — Matthew 12:27.

CHAPTER SEVENTEEN: Letter to the Sovereign, HM (1926 – 2022).

Their indiscreetly weaponised legal system.

Creeping Ukraine.

Creeping DPRK.

"Ethical foreign policy." Robin Cook (1946–2005).

If Masons are as clever, and as ethical, and as righteous, and as brave as they imply, why didn't they foresee that Putin will steal Crimea, and why did they look away while he did?

Half-educated school drop-outs and their superiors who have informal access to some very, very, powerful white Freemason Judges — Habakkuk 1:4.

BEDFORD, ENGLAND: GDC, Freemason, Brother, Richard William Hill (NHS Postgraduate Tutor), unrelentingly lied under oath — Habakkuk 1:4.

A very, very, dishonest NHS Postgraduate Tutor of our Empire of Stolen Affluence — Habakkuk.

A racist crooked Freemason. Integrity, Friendship, Respect, and Charity: All for one, and one for all.

Might former Judge, Negress Constance Briscoe have 'WALKED', when she wilfully misled the Police — had she been Caucasian, English, Male, and Freemason?

BEDFORD, ENGLAND: Your Majesty in Heaven, near our Father in Heaven sed on cogent, irrefutable, and available evidence, GDC, Sue Gregory, Officer of the Most Excellent Order of our Empire (OBE), unrelentingly lied under implied oath – Habakkuk 1:4.

A very, very, dishonest white woman.

A closeted hereditary racist crooked Officer of the Most Excellent Order of our Empire of Stolen Affluence – Habakkuk

Your Majesty, before hereditary RACIAL HATRED unravels, it is always conspiracy theory, and when Christ unravels it, it instantly mutates to a conspiracy.

Your Majesty, Civil Procedures Rules, Statute, Precedent are baren exercises in Jurisdictions where verdicts Freemasons prior agreed, in Freemasons Temples, must be realised by hook or by crook, including via the employment of incompetent mendacity, and absolutely everything else is confidence trickery and deceit – Habakkuk 1:4

Your Majesty, then, their bastardised, indiscreetly dishonest, unashamedly mediocre, vindictive, potently weaponised, and institutionally racist legal system was overseen by closeted white supremacist Freemason Judges – Habakkuk 1:4.

Your Majesty, there is absolutely NOTHING closeted white supremacist bastards cannot do to our people (Africans), and as they are very, very, highly civilised, and super-enlightened, they adhere very, very, strictly to the rule of law, and they do everything 'legally'.

What exactly is the meaning of 'legally' - in Jurisdictions where no one is good – Psalm 53, and where almost everyone, including Judges, tells incompetent racist lies, and all the time – Habakkuk 1:4?

"Lies are told all the time." Sir Michael Havers (1923 – 1992), Attorney General, 1980.

BEDFORD, ENGLAND: District Judge Paul Robert Ayers, > 70, a Mason, and the Senior Vice President of the Association of Her Majesty's District Judges, of 3, St Paul's Square, MK 40 1SQ, the Nigerian is irreconcilably very, very, different from you and your type because the mind he got, unsolicited, is considerably finer than the legal system you serve, and it is possible to use cogent facts and irrefutable evidence to irreversibly destroy you and it. You will find the disclosure very worrying, so to protect you, and more, in pursuant of self-preservation, it is safer to conceal the truth from hereditary ignorant and shallow closeted white supremacist bastards, as when 33% God, disclosed pictures His infinite mind painted, He was lynched like Gadhafi and crucified, at only 33.

Bedford's District Judge, Paul Robert Ayers, > 70, a Mason, and the Senior Vice President of the Association of Her Majesty's District Judges, of 3, St Paul's Square, MK 40 1SQ: White man, let me tell you, reasoning and vision do not have finite boundaries, and the fellow told only truths when He disclosed pictures His unbounded mind painted. It is a scary, but it is the absolute truth that the supernatural exists, and it is consistently accessible all those who stand where He can come, not through righteousness, but only through unalloyed faith, and His unsolicited and undeserved kindness – Romans 11.

Bedford's District Judge, Paul Robert Ayers, > 70, a Mason, and the Senior Vice President of the Association of Her Majesty's District Judges, of 3, St Paul's Square, MK 40 1SQ: White man, let me tell you, sadly we are all FORKED, as His Knights attacks all Kings and Queens simultaneously, and only Queens can move. White man, let me tell you, we are all travelling in the wrong direction, as every mind that is not aligned with the notion of infinite reasoning and vision – is not aligned to the discernible exceptionalism of the fellow – John 14:6, which the sole basis of 'The Faith' – in 'the Defender of the Faith', is travelling in the wrong direction, and heading straight for the rocks. "

"It does no harm to throw the occasional man overboard, but it does not do much good if you are steering full speed ahead for the rocks." Sir Ian Gilmour (1926 – 2007).

Bedford's District Judge Paul Robert Ayers, > 70, a Mason, and the Senior Vice President of the Association of Her Majesty's District Judges, of 3, St Paul's Square, MK 40 1SQ, white man, let me tell you, the Nigerian is foetus, as what He can vividly see is clearer than dreams, visions, and prophesies – Act 2:17.

Bedford's District Judge, Paul Robert Ayers, > 70, a Mason, and the Senior Vice President of the Association of Her Majesty's District Judges, of 3, St Paul's Square, MK 40 1SQ, white man, let me tell you, sincere immodesty is sincerer than insincere modesty, believe me, white man, based on several decades very, very, proximate observations and direct experiences, your whiteness is your most valuable asset as a human being, and you neither made nor chose it (pure chance), and without it, you are froth -PURIFIED NOTHING.

They see Senior District Judge Paul Robert Ayers, > 70, a Mason, and the Senior Vice President of the Association of Her Majesty's District Judges, of 3, St Paul's Square, MK 40 1SQ, but the Nigerian sees a poly-educated hereditary racist white imbecile bastard, and if they aren't excessively stupid, the Nigerian must be mad.

"To disagree with three – fourths of the British public on all points is one of the first elements of sanity, one of the deepest consolations in all moments of spiritual doubt." Wilde

Bedford's District Judge Paul Robert Ayers, > 70, a Mason, and the Senior Vice President of the Association of Her Majesty's District Judges, of 3, St Paul's Square, MK 40 1SQ, white man, let me tell you, you are verifiably recklessly sloppy, unashamedly incompetent, maliciously dishonest, unapologetically and indiscreetly white supremacist thug, and/or thoroughly confused – Habakkuk 1:4. Alzheimer's disease is considerably more common than ordinarily realises, and it colour-blind, and it should be incompatible with the competent administration of

English Law, and the competent administration of English should be an inviolable basic right.

OYINBO ODE: OYINBO OLODO: Bedford's District Judge Paul Robert Ayers, > 70, a Mason, and the Senior Vice President of the Association of Her Majesty's District Judges, of 3, St Paul's Square, MK 40 1SQ, apart from debt-collection, what was in Norwich for functional semi-illiterate white Solicitors (disproportionately but not exclusively white), including Poly-educated 5th Rate Partners, to do?

Your Majesty, English Law is equal for Caucasians and Africans, but its administration isn't, and the latter is the 'meat', and sadly, it's closeted hereditary white supremacist tyrants' tool.

"Rightful liberty is unobstructed action according to our will within limits drawn around us by the equal rights of others. I do not add 'within the limits of the law' because law is often but the tyrant's will, and always so when it violates the rights of the individual." President Thomas Jefferson

"Affluence is not a birth right." David Cameron

Your Majesty, based on available evidence, a British Premier openly implied that he had very good reasons to suspect that white Judges (disproportionately but not exclusively white) are institutionally RACIST.

Facts are sacred.

"All sections of UK society are institutionally racist." Sir Bernard Hogan-Howe, KBE, a former Metropolitan Chief.

English Judiciary and its Principal Officers, all white Judges (disproportionately but not exclusively white) – are parts of UK society.

"British Prime Minister attacks racial bias in Universities and the Justice System. 'David Cameron has persuaded a leading labour MP to 'defect' by launching a government investigation into why black people make up such a high proportion of the prison population. Mr Cameron said Mr Lammy would examine why blacks and ethnic minorities make up nearly a quarter of Crown Court defendants – compared to 14 percent of the population. He added: 'If you are black, you are more likely to be in a prison cell than studying in a university. And if you are black, it seems you're more likely to be sentenced to custody for a crime than if you are white. 'We should investigate why this is and how we can end this possible discrimination. That's why I have asked David Lammy to lead a review. Mr Lammy, who is a qualified barrister, said: 'I am pleased to accept the Prime Minister's invitation." Mr Paul Dacre, Daily Mail, 31.01.2016.

Judges are not SAINTS, they are fallible mere mortals like the rest of us, and their appointments are not based on progressive, fairer, colour-blind and measurable objectivity, had that been the case, the issue of diversity would not have arisen.

Many fallible human beings are RACISTS.

Only stupid black people believe that they became equal to white people – under their law, after the 1807 Act, and only stupider Negroes expect white Freemason Judges to measure their own white kindred with the same yardsticks they use to measure descendants and/or mere Africans (African Bombata), and only the stupidest among Negurs expect demons to cast out demons – Matthew 12:27.

WHITE PRIVILEGE: Ignorant racist leeches; ultra-righteous descendants of industrial-scale professional WHITE THIEVES and owners of stolen poor black children of defenceless Africans, including the African ancestors of Meghan Markle's white children - Habakkuk.

Facts are sacred.

Homogeneity in the administration of their law is the impregnable secure mask of merciless racist evil – Habakkuk 1:4.

JUDICIAL DIVERSITY: ACCELERATING CHANGE.
Sir Geoffrey Bindman, KC, and Karon Monaghan, KC.
"The near absence of women and Black, Asian and minority ethnic judges in the senior judiciary, is no longer tolerable. It undermines the democratic legitimacy of our legal system; it demonstrates a denial of fair and equal opportunities to members of underrepresented groups, and the diversity deficit weakens the quality of justice."

GDC: "They may not have been well written from a grammatical point of view...." Dr Geraint Evans, Postgraduate Tutor, Oxford, of Rowtree Dental Care, Rowtree Road, Northampton NN4 0NY.

A brainless closeted hereditary racist crooked Welsh bastard.

"The earth contains to race of human beings so totally vile and worthless as the Welsh ...." Walter Savage Landor.

OYINBO ODE: OYINBO OLODO.
"Sir, he was dull in company, dull in his closet, dull everywhere. He was dull in a new way, and that made many people think him GREAT. He was a mechanical poet." Dr Samuel Johnson

GDC: Apart from creating very, very, cushy salaried jobs for white Solicitors and Barristers who FAILED in practice (quasi-communism), and loads did, what does crooked closeted hereditary racist Welsh imbecile, Dr Geraint Evans, Postgraduate Tutor, Oxford, of Rowtree Dental Care, Rowtree Road, Northampton NN4 0NY, need very, very, expensive administration of English Law.

OECD and Dr Richard Dawkins implied that all the children of Dr Geraint Evans, Postgraduate Tutor, Oxford, of Rowtree Dental Care, Rowtree Road, Northampton NN4 0NY, should be duller than their crooked, hereditary racist patriarch.

"Natural selection will not remove ignorance from future generations." Dr Richard Dawkins.

Adults with the basic skills of a foetus will succeed imbeciles (adults with the basic skills of a child), and the former will need food and shelter, not very, very, expensive administration of English Law.
"Why, Sir, Sherry is dull, naturally dull; but it must have taken him a great deal of pains to become what we now see him. Such an excess of stupidity, Sir, is not in Nature." Dr Samuel Johnson

CHAPTER EIGHTEEN: Letter to the Sovereign, HM (1926 – 2022).

Integrity. Friendship. Respect. Charity.

Slimy indiscreetly deceptive brainless nonsense.

Your Majesty, then, and only there, members of the very, very, charitable Antichrist closeted Freemasonry Quasi-Religion (Mediocre Mafia, New Pharisees, New Good Samaritans, Defenders of Faiths, including all the religions and faiths associated with the 15 Holy Books in the House of Commons, and Dissenters of the Faith – Johnson 14:6), find a very, very, dull white man, and they adorn him with one or two fancy titles (Postgraduate Tutor, Oxford), and he becomes their Zombie Private Soldier.

NORTHAMPTON, ENGLAND: Based on available evidence, GDC-WITNESS, Dr Geraint Evans, Postgraduate Tutor, Oxford, of Rowtree Dental Care, Rowtree Road, Northampton NN4 0NY unrelentingly lied under implied oath - Habakkuk 1:4; John 8:44; John 10:10.

A CLOSETED RACIST WHITE WELSH IMBECILE CROOK.

"Find the truth and tell it." Harold Pinter

CREEPING DPRK.

The ancestors of Kim did not kidnap and imprison all the people of North Korea, overnight, they did very, very, gradually, and over decades, and the basic right to disclose pictures painted by free minds – was the first to be withdrawn, and the mind was the first to be gaoled.

There is Freedom of Expression in DPRK, there, one is free to say only what Kim wants to hear.

In some parts of the world, one is free to say only what Freemasons and Globalists want to hear.
Your Majesty, had GDC, Sue Gregory, Officer of the Most Excellent Order of our Empire (OBE) been black, or had the Judges been black, the crooked racist cougar, albeit an Officer of the Most Excellent Order of our Empire – would have been in trouble – Habakkuk 1:4.

Your Majesty, some black people truly believe that former Judge Constance Briscoe might have 'WALKED' had she been male, Caucasian, genetic English, and a member of the Antichrist closeted white supremacist Freemasonry Quasi-Religion (

Your Majesty, then, and only there, members of the very, very, charitable Antichrist Closeted White Supremacist Freemasonry Quasi-Religion (Mediocre Mafia, New Pharisees, New Good Samaritans, Defenders of Faiths, including all the Faiths associated with the 15 Holy Books in the House of Commons, and Dissenters of the Faith – John 14:6), adorned their wives, or concubines of the members, friends, and families, including mere dmf, with very, very, High Titles (Gongs), and they became Charitable Freemasons Zombie Private Soldiers: Conflict of interest complicated by nepotism.

BEDFORD, ENGLAND: Your Majesty, based on cogent, irrefutable, and available evidence, GDC, Sue Gregory, Officer of the Most Excellent Order of our Empire (OBE), unrelentingly lied under implied oath – Habakkuk 1:4.

A very, very, dishonest white woman.

A racist crooked Officer of the Most Excellent Order of our Empire of Stolen Affluence – Habakkuk

If all the Freemasons in Bedfordshire, including all the Freemason Judges, and all the 33rd Degree Freemasons at the Bedfordshire Masonic Centre, the Keep, Bedford Road, Kempston, MK42 AH, could use cogent facts and irrefutable evidence to disprove the truth that GDC, Sue Gregory, Officer of the Most Excellent Order of our Empire (OBE), unrelentingly lied under implied oath, and if they could use cogent facts and irrefutable evidence to disprove the truth that GDC, Shiv Pabary, Member of the Most Excellent Order of our Empire (MBE), Justice of Peace, and the archetypal GDC Committee Chairman (Uncle Tom), unrelentingly lied under implied oath, and if they could use cogent facts and irrefutable evidence to disprove the truth that GDC, Mrs Helen Falcon, Member of the Most Excellent Order of our Empire (MBE), a former Member of the GDC Committee, a Rotarian (auxiliary Freemason), a former Postgraduate Dean, Oxford, and the spouse of Mr Falcon, they will confirm the belief of scores of millions of Britons, which is that Antichrist closeted white supremacist Freemasonry Quasi-Religion (Mediocre Mafia, New Pharisees, New Good Samaritans, Defenders of Faiths, including all faiths and religions associated with the 15 Holy Books in the House of Commons, and Dissenters of the Faith – John 14:6), Antichrist Islam, and Antichrist Judaism, and all other motley assemblies of exotic religions and faiths under the common umbrella of the Governor of the Church of England, the Defender of the Faith – John 14:6, are not intellectually flawed Satanic Mumbo Jumbo, and they will confirm that reasoning and vision have finite boundaries, and if it could be proved that that reasoning and vision are finite, it will confirm that the fellow lied when, before Jews and Romans, in the Council, He disclosed pictures His purportedly infinite mind painted, and He must have also lied when He audaciously stated He was exceptional – John 14:6.

Your Majesty, based on cogent, irrefutable, and available evidence, closeted hereditary white supremacist privileged dullards are thoroughly crazy, and the white imbeciles (predominantly but not exclusively white adults with the basic skills of a child) they shepherd do not know – because they are crazier, as the legal system they serve, is verifiably based on incompetent RACIST LIES – Habakkuk 1:4.

Based on several decades of very, very, proximate observations, direct experiences, and available evidence, in jurisdictions where verdicts prior agreed, secretly, in Freemasons' Temples must be realised in open courts, civil procedure rules, statute, and precedent are baren exercises: Incompetent art incompetently imitates life.

BEDFORD, ENGLAND: GDC, Freemason, Brother, Richard William Hill (NHS Postgraduate Tutor) fabricated reports and unrelentingly lied under oath — Habakkuk 1:4.

A very, very, dishonest white man.

A crooked racist postgraduate tutor of our Empire of Stolen Affluence — Habakkuk.

CONFLICT OF INTEREST: Before the RACIST CRIMES of closeted hereditary white supremacist Freemasons unravel, they are always conspiracy theories, and when Christ unravels them, they instantly mutate to mistakes. WHITE PRIVILEGE: If one is a crooked racist white bastard, and if one has unbounded and unaccountable power, it is natural that one will use such power to justify hereditary RACIAL HATRED, and if one cannot justify innate racial intolerance, one will try to bury it, and if one cannot bury it, one will destroy the witness, as the loose end must be tied by hook or by crook — the Negrophobic charade SHOW must go on.

Matthew 14: John was jailed only because he spoke the truth, but the very, very, intolerant lunatic Jew, King Herod, removed his head, and he was not punished for speaking, John was decapitated solely to permanently prevent him from speaking.

Closeted hereditary white supremacist bastards want superiority, but they don't want Freedom of Expression, because they don't want their mentally gentler children, and the white imbeciles they shepherd (predominantly but not exclusively white adults with the basic skills of a child) to know that their self-awarded supreme knowledge is baseless and brainless, and the centuries-old unspoken myth that the universally acknowledged irrefutably superior skin colour that the very, very, fortunate wearer neither made nor chose — is related to intellect, is the mother of all racist scams.

They are not the only creations of Almighty God, and they are not immortal, and the universally acknowledged irrefutably superior skin colour that they neither made nor chose is not the only wonder of our common world.

White Supremacy and White Privilege are conjoined twins: Racist monsters with two heads, one body, two fertility tools, and four legs, and the four legs travel in the same direction, as they must do.
They hate us, and we know. Motivated by uncontrollable hereditary RACIAL HATRED, they maliciously economically strangulate us, not to punish us for a particular offense, or to protect and preserve the public interest, they do in pursuant of tampering with our minds, and killing us, albeit hands-off, and tie the loose ends of the properly organised racist crimes that Christ has unravelled.

Google: Dr Richard Bamgboye, GP.

Google: Dr Anand Kamath, Dentist.

Richard and Anand's minds were overwhelmed with incompetent racist lies, and they were killed by closeted hereditary white supremacist thugs, albeit hands-off.

They were racist murderers, but the hid the mens rea in the belly of actus reus; they tampered with the minds of innocent foreigners, and they murdered them, albeit hands.

Dr Richard Bamgboye, GP and Dr Anand Kamath, Dentist, came to Great Britain for a better life, but closeted hereditary white supremacist bastards – prematurely sent them to the afterlife. Their racist killers are not immortal, so they shall go to them – 2 Samuel 12:23.

"The most potent weapon in the hand of the oppressor is the mind of the oppressed." Steve Biko (1946–1977).

Only our people (foreigners) are dying in this latent, but very, very, potent — undeclared RACE WAR.

"He is a typical Englishman, usually violent and always dull."

They are very, very, hardened racist criminals, and closeted white supremacist Freemason Judges seem to be in the loop, and all loose end must be tied, as their children and white imbeciles they shepherd (predominantly but not exclusively white adults with the basic skills of a child), must not know that they are very, very, hardened racist criminals, and including some closeted hereditary white supremacist Freemason Judges, and the world must not know that their so called 'rule of law' is an institutionalised Negrophobic charade that is more crooked and corrupt that what is obtainable in Zelensky's Ukraine.

Scotland, England: GDC, Kevin Atkinson (Scottish Kev), our Postgraduate Tutor, Oxford, unrelentingly lied under oath — Habakkuk 1:4.

A very, very, dishonest Scotsman.

Our racist crooked Postgraduate Tutor, Oxford, of our Empire of Stolen Affluence — Habakkuk.

Babies with gigantic uranium mines near their huts eat only 1.5/day in Niger, West Africa, a scatter-head, crooked, and racist Scotsman whose mentally gentler white children mightn't be able to spell uranium, and whose white Scottish ancestors, including the white Scottish ancestors of Sean Connery (1930–2020), were fed like battery hens with yields of stolen poor black children of defenceless Africans, including the African ancestors of the great grandchildren of the Duke of Edinburgh of blessed memory (1921–2021), is our Helen Falcon's Scottish Postgraduate Tutor, Oxford.

Google: Helen Falcon, Racist Empress.

Philippian 1:21: Was Phillip a 33rd Degree Freemason, Scottish Rite?
An ignorant racist Scottish crook.

An ultra-righteous descendant of industrialised-scale professional thieves, extremely nasty, and mercilessly vicious racist murderers, and owners of stolen poor children of defenceless Africans, including the West African ancestors of the white children of Meghan Markle.

Based on available evidence, Meghan Markle is 43% West African (Nigerian).

"Time for Scots to say sorry for slavery. Herald Scotland: Ian Bell, Columnist / Sunday 28 April 2013 / Opinion. According to the American founding father, the son of a Caithness Kirk's Minister had about him "an air of great simplicity and honesty'". The likes of James Boswell and Laurence Sterne also enjoyed the merchant's company.. To his contemporaries, he was, as the author Adam Hochschild has written, "'a wise, thoughtful man who embodied the Scottish virtues of frugality, sobriety, and hard work'". Oswald was a scholar of theology, philosophy, and history. He collected art, particularly Rubens and Rembrandt, and gave handsomely to charity. Oswald, who learned his trade in Glasgow, also represented Britain in negotiations with the Americans after their war of liberation. He was the cosmopolitan epitome of Enlightenment success. But when he wasn't busy with good works, Oswald waded in blood. The precise number of deaths that can be laid at his door is impossible to calculate. As the leading figure in Grant, Oswald & Co, he had investments in each corner of the "'triangular trade'". In his own name, Oswald trafficked at least 13,000 Africans, although he never set foot on their continent. By the time he bought Auchincruive House and

100,000 acres in Ayrshire in 1764, he was worth £500,000.
Writing in 2005, Hochschild thought this was ""roughly
equivalent"" to $68 million (about £44m). This is
conservative. Oswald was remarkable, but not unique. Where
Glasgow and its merchants in sugar, tobacco, and human life
are concerned, there are plenty of names and no shortage of
monuments: Dennistoun, Campbell, Glassford, Cochrane,
Buchanan, Hamilton, Bogle, Ewing, Donald, Speirs, Dunlop.
One way to understand what they wrought is simple: take
pleasure in the city''s architecture today and you are likely to
be admiring the fruits of slavery. Glasgow is not alone in
that. London, Liverpool and Bristol also have their stories to
tell. Edinburgh's once-great banks grew from foundations
built on bones. The first Scottish venture into slavery set out
from the capital in 1695. Montrose, Dumfries, Greenock and
Port Glasgow each tried their hands. In the language of the
present age, they were all in it together. When commerce was
coursing around the triangle, most of polite Scotland was
implicated. The nobility (and country) rendered bankrupt in
1700 in the aftermath of the Darien Venture was by the mid-
1760s contemplating big, elegant townhouses and 100,000-
acre estates. You could call that a reversal of fortune.
Contrary to self-serving myth, it did not happen because of
"'frugality, sobriety, and hard work". Certain things need to
be remembered about Scotland and slavery. One is that the
mercantile class got stinking rich twice over: despite fortunes
made from stolen lives, they were quick to demand
compensation when slavery was ended in 1833. Britain's
government decided that £20m, a staggering sum, could be
raised. In his 2010 book, The Price of Emancipation,
Nicholas Draper reckons Glasgow's mob got £400,000 — in

modern terms, hundreds of millions. Compensation cases also demonstrated that Scots were not merely following an English lead. According to Draper, a country with 10% of the British population accounted for at least 15% of absentee slavers. By another estimate, 30% of Jamaican plantations were run by Scots. For all the pride taken in the abolitionist societies of Glasgow and Edinburgh, the slaveholders did not suffer because of abolition. They were "'compensated'". And that wasn't the worst of it. Thanks to Hollywood movies, the slave economy of the American South is still taken as barbarism's benchmark. Few realise that the behaviour of Scots busy getting rich in the slaveholders'' empire was actually worse — routinely worse — than the worst of the cottonocracy. You need only count the corpses……………"

GIGANTIC yield of millions of stolen African children, including the African ancestors of Meghan Markle's white children, not feudal agriculture, lured Jews, including the ancestors of Benjamin Disraeli (1804–1881), to Great Britain. Before Slavery, what?

Then, there was only subsistence feudal agriculture.

"Agriculture not only gives riches to a nation, but the only one she can call her own." Dr Samuel Johnson (1709 – 1784).

CHAPTER NINETEEN: Dr Ngozi Ekweremadu, a Nigerian whistleblower.

BEDFORD, ENGLAND: GDC, Sue Gregory, Officer of the Most Excellent Order of our Empire (OBE), unrelentingly lied under implied oath — Habakkuk 1:4.

A very, very, dishonest white woman.

Our crooked closeted hereditary racist Officer of the Most Excellent Order of our Empire of Stolen Affluence — Habakkuk.

OYINBO OLE: Then, armed greedy racist white bastards and those they armed – carried and sold millions of stolen poor black children of defenceless Africans, including the African ancestors of Meghan Markle's white children, now, they steal natural resources from our own Africa - Habakkuk.

Substitution is fraudulent emancipation.

"Moderation is a virtue only among those who are thought to have found alternatives." Henry Kissinger

BEDFORD, ENGLAND: District Judge Paul Robert Ayers, > 70, a Mason, and Senior Vice President of the Association of Her Majesty's District Judges, 3, St Paul's

Square, MK40 1SQ, let me tell you, you are worthy only because your universally acknowledged irrefutably superior whiteness and because England is very, very, rich, apart from those, you are PURIFIED NOTHING.
Affluence was preceded by SLAVERY. Prior to Slavery, there weren't very, very, many proper houses in KEMPSTON.

BEDFORD, ENGLAND: District Judge Paul Robert Ayers, > 70, a Mason, and Senior Vice President of the Association of Her Majesty's District Judges, 3, St Paul's Square, MK40 1SQ: Our own money, NIGERIA (oil/gas), is by far more relevant to the economic survival of your white spouse, your white father, your white mother, and all white children than Mason's Kempston: OYINBO OLE.

Our ignorant descendant of ultra-righteous WHITE THIEVES and owners of stolen poor black children of defenceless AFRICANS, including the African ancestors of Meghan Markle's white children – Habakkuk.

Facts are sacred.

No brain.
Poor in natural resources.
Several centuries of stealing and slavery preceded the huge STOLEN TRUST FUND
Only their superior skin colour and Almighty God are truly good – Mark 10:18, and they neither made nor chose it.

"The best opportunity of developing academically and emotional." Bedford's District Judge Paul Robert Ayers, >70, a Mason, and the Senior Vice President of the Association of Her Majesty's District Judges, 3, St Paul's Square, MK40 1SQ, proofed-read and approved Judgement.

Brainless nonsense.

"To survive, you must tell stories …… I believe that what we become depends on what our fathers teach us at odd moments, when they aren't trying to teach us. We are formed by little scraps of wisdom." Umberto Eco

Bedford's District Judge Paul Robert Ayers, >70, a Mason, and the Senior Vice President of the Association of Her Majesty's District Judges, 3, St Paul's Square, MK40 1SQ: Our semi-illiterate racist white dunce approved what his functional semi-illiterate white mother and father spoke (deductible), the type of stories his white father used to tell when he returned home from QUEEN VICTORIA, at odd hours, and thoroughly stoned, and which his poly-educated white supervisors and superiors in LUTON authorised.

HHJ Perusko studied law at Poly: Not Russell Group Inferior Education – Proverbs 17:16.

Our own NIGERIA: Shell's docile cash cow since 1956.

Our own Nigerian babies with huge oil wells and gas fields near their huts eat only 1.5/day, a very, very, bellyful closeted hereditary racist white bastard whose white mother and father have never seen crude oil, and whose white ancestors, including ultra-righteous John Bunyan (1628 – 1688), were fed like battery hens with yields of stolen poor black children of defenceless Africans, including the African ancestors of Meghan Markle's white children was our District Judge in BEDFORD, Great Britain, what's great about sh*t?

BEDFORD, ENGLAND: District Judge Paul Robert Ayers, >70, a Mason, and the Senior Vice President of the Association of Her Majesty's District Judges, 3, St Paul's Square, MK40 1SQ,which part of our Grand Cathedral Court, 3, St Paul's Square, MK40 1SQ,wasn't STOLEN, or which part of it is the yield of the Higher IQs of your own white mother and father, or which part of it preceded SLAVERY: The building or its chattels?

The very, very, greedy, murderous, Scottish racist bastards are no longer here, but it will be very, very, naive not to expect their mutant genes of sadism and savagery to continue to flow through the veins of their direct descendants who remain here.

If there are cogent, irrefutable, and available evidence that one's white Scottish ancestors were extremely nasty racist murderers, armed robbers, armed land grabbers, gun runners, drug dealers (opium merchants), industrial-scale professional THIEVES of movable and immovable valuable assets belonging to others, and merchants of stolen lives of very, very, poor black children of defenceless Africans, including the African ancestors of Meghan Markle's white children, it will be very, very, naive not to expect RACIAL HATRED to be part of one's genetic inheritances.

It is not the truth that RACIAL HATRED is extinct, and it not a myth, and it is considerably more common than ordinarily realised.

"White supremacist is real, and it needs to be shattered." Dr Cornel West.

We are who we are, the inheritors of the genes of our individual ancestors, and no one should pay for visible and invisible genetic characteristics that they neither made nor chose.

"The white man is the devil." Mohammed Ali (1942–2016).

Based on several decades of very, very, proximate observations and direct experiences, the white man is not only a devil, but he is also a THIEF.

"Many Scots masters were considered among the most brutal, with life expectancy on their plantations averaging a mere four years. We worked them to death then simply imported more to keep the sugar and thus the money flowing. Unlike centuries of grief and murder, an apology cost nothing. So, what does Scotland have to say?" Herald Scotland: Ian Bell, Columnist, Sunday 28 April 2013.

Ignorance is bliss.

"As hard hearted as a Scot of Scotland." English saying.

"The white man is the devil." Elijah Mohammed (1897–1975).

If there are cogent, irrefutable, and available evidence that the white ancestors of one's white mother and father were THIEVES and owners of stolen poor black children of defenceless Africans, including the African ancestors of Meghan Markle's white children, it will be very, very, naive not to expect RACIAL HATRED complicated by incompetent mendacity to be part of one's genetic inheritances — Habakkuk.

"Of black men, the numbers are too great who are now repining under English cruelty." Dr Samuel Johnson BEDFORD, ENGLAND: GDC, Freemason, Brother Richard Hill (NHS) fabricated reports and unrelentingly lied under oath.

The statement of withdrawal of an incompetent NHS racist fabrication, which was probably created by the Freemasonry Fraternity, was based on incompetent RACIST LIES – Habakkuk 1:4.

Very, very, powerful, and vulgarly charitable Freemasonry Quasi-Religion (Mediocre Mafia, New Pharisees, New Good Samaritans, Defenders of Faiths, including all the Faiths and Religions associated with the 15 Holy books in the House of Commons, and Dissenter of the Faith – John 14:6) - are quasi-demigods, but they are not our Gods.

"We have the power to turn against our creators." Dr Richard Dawkins.

CONFLICT OF INTEREST: The creators of WHITE IMBECILES (predominantly but not exclusively white adults with the basic skills of a child) punish self-educated Africans who can't relate to imbecility.

https://www.youtube.com/watch?v=BlpH4hG7m1A&feature=youtu.be

"They may not have been well written from a grammatical point of view, but I am confident I had not forgotten any of the facts." Dr Geraint Evans, Postgraduate Tutor, Oxford

https://youtu.be/rayVcfyu9Tw

Dr Rowan Williams was very suspicious of the Builders: Charitable Mediocre Mafia.

Based on available evidence, the Grand Masonic Temple to Baal, 60 Great Queen St, Holborn, London WC2B 5AZ, was built in London, in the 1700s, at a height of the barbarously racist traffic in millions of stolen children of defenceless poor people - Habakkuk.

They do indiscreet and vulgar Pharisees' charitable works in exchange for what?

Then, theirs was not a good deal, and now, theirs isn't a good deal – Matthew 4:9.

Freemason, Brother Jimmy Savile did not fix anything for NOTHING.

Antichrist Racist Freemasons: Charitable half-educated school dropouts and their superiors who have informal access to some very powerful white Judges – Habakkuk 1:4.

"I think I will ask our legal adviser for any advice he may have. My view is that there are six or seven of us here who had the admission down, but we cannot find it in the transcript and there is wordings that imply that there was, but it is not in black and white….." Shiv Pabary, MBE, Member of the Most Excellent Order of our Empire, Justice of Peace, and Archetypal GDC Committee Chairman.

A very, very, dishonest scatter-head Indian.

Our Indian. Our uncle Tom.

"One witness at a Royal Commission in 1897 said that the ambition of Indians in Trinidad was, 'to buy a cow, then a shop, and say: "We are no Nigg*rs to work in cane fields." Patrick French — 'The World Is What It Is, The Authorised Biography of V.S. Naipaul.

Based on available evidence, Shiv Pabary, MBE, Member of the Most Excellent Order of our Empire, Justice of Peace, and Archetypal GDC Committee Chairman., and our very, very, dishonest scatter-head Indian (Uncle Tom), maliciously lied or he was recklessly confused when he stated, "I think I will ask our legal adviser for any advice he may have. My view is that there are six or seven of us here who had the admission down …." Their Indian also lied incompetently or he was thoroughly confused when he stated, "….. but we cannot find it in the transcript ……" Shiv Pabary, MBE, Member of the Most Excellent Order of our Empire, Justice of Peace, and Archetypal GDC Committee Chairman, a very, very, dishonest scatter-head Indian (uncle Tom), was incompetently dishonest and/or thoroughly confused when the stated, "……but it is not in black and white….."

A brainless, scatter-head, crooked, and racist Indian: Uncle Tom.

If words were written down, and they were not in black and white, they must be in red, gold, black, and green.

"Rally round the red gold black and green. …….. How can we sing in a strange land. Don't want to sing in a strange land" Steel Pulse.

The report, by the OECD, warns that the UK needs to take significant action to boost the basic skills of the nation's young people. The 460-page study is based on the first-ever survey of the literacy, numeracy and problem-solving at work skills of 16 to 65-year-olds in 24 countries, with almost 9,000 people taking part in England and Northern Ireland to make up the UK results. The findings showed that England and Northern Ireland have some of the highest proportions of adults scoring no higher than Level 1 in literacy and numeracy — the lowest level on the OECD's scale. This suggests that their skills in the basics are no better than that of a 10-year-old.

AN IMBECILE: AN ADULT WITH THE BASIC SKILLS OF A CHILD.

Very, very, accurate seers: They foresaw that Britons, not all, will be imbeciles (adults with the basic skills of a child), so they embarked on armed robbery and dispossession raids in AFRICA. Wherever, armed racist, greedy white bastards, and those they armed, mercilessly slaughtered AFRICANS, they dispossessed them, and whenever they robbed Africans, they took possession, and they used yields of several continuous centuries of the greediest economic cannibalism and the evilest racist terrorism the world will ever know – Habakkuk, to create lavishly social security system for white imbeciles (predominantly but not exclusively white adults with the basic skills of a child), and they decommissioned natural selection, and they reversed evolution, and they made it possible for millions of imbeciles of all shades (adults with the basic skills of a child) to breed more millions of imbeciles of all shades.

What exactly is the point of Civil Procedure Rules (pr), Statute, and precedent – in an institutionally racist legal that seems to be overseen by Freemasons, and where white people, only white people, including a white Welsh imbecile,

Closeted hereditary white supremacist bastards know to steal for white imbeciles, but they do not know how to repair the scatter-heads of their own white kindred.

Apart from creating very, very, cushy salaried jobs for white Solicitors and Barristers (predominantly but not exclusively white) who couldn't hack it in the very competitive real world, loads couldn't, and didn't (quasi-communism), what do white imbeciles (predominantly but not exclusively white adults with the basic skills of a child) need very expensive administration of English law for?

"Natural selection will not remove ignorance from future generations." Dr Richard Dawkins.

Adults with the basic skills of a foetus will succeed adults with the basic skills of a child (imbeciles), and the former will need only food and shelter, not very, very, expensive administration of English Law.

In the near future, colour-blind AI, not closeted hereditary white supremacist Freemason Judges, will settle disputes among white imbeciles (predominantly but not exclusively white adults with the basic skills of a child) – Habakkuk 1:4.

CHAPTER TWENTY: Letter to the Sovereign, HM (1926 – 2022).

"We have the power to turn against our creators." Dr Richard Dawkins.

Then, and only there, all Judges were white, and most of them were Freemasons, and some of them were thicker than a gross of planks, and white Freemason Judges who believed that daily dialogues with white imbeciles (predominantly but not exclusively white adults with the basic skills of a child) were worthwhile and manly, were scammers, and white Freemason Judges who demanded and accepted very, very, valuable considerations in exchange for daily dialogues with white imbeciles (predominantly but not exclusively white adults with the basic skills of a child) were racketeers (THIEVES) — Habakkuk.

If all the Gods in India, loads of them, and all the 33rd Degree Freemasons (Scottish Rite), at Byker Masonic Hall Corbridge Road, Byker, Newcastle upon Tyne, Tyne and Wear, NE6 1HY, and all Freemason Lodges and Halls in Newcastle and Wear, could disprove the truth that Shiv Pabary, MBE, Member of the Most Excellent Order of our Empire, Justice of Peace, and Archetypal GDC Committee Chairman, a very, very, dishonest scatter-head Indian (uncle Tom), was incompetently dishonest and/or thoroughly confused, and unrelentingly lied under oath (on record), they will confirm the belief of millions of people in Great Britain and in India, which is that Antichrist Freemasonry Quasi-Religion (Mediocre Mafia, New Pharisees, New Good Samaritan, Defenders of Faiths, including all the faiths and religions associated with the 15 Holy Books in the House of Commons, and Dissenter of the Faith — John 14:6) and all other exotic faiths and religions under the common umbrella of the Governor of the Church of England, and the Defender of the Faith — John 14:6, aren't intellectually flawed Satanic Mumbo Jumbo, and they will also confirm that reasoning and vision have finite boundaries, and if reasoning and vision have finite boundaries, He must have lied when He purportedly disclosed pictures His unbounded mind painted, and He must have also lied when He audaciously stated that He was Divine, Exceptional, and Immortal. "The first quality that is needed is audacity." Churchill. If one's skin colour is universally acknowledged to be irrefutably superior, and if one's intellect is not, it is plainly deductible that Freedom of Expression is not one's friend.

"Sorry, I am a free speech absolutist." Elon Musk.
 Some crooked racist white bastards (predominantly but not exclusively white) will be able to sleep soundly when the loose ends are tied.

Once you can see them, you have reached the end of your life, as the loose ends must be tied, and the white imbeciles they shepherd (predominantly but not exclusively white adults with the basic skills of a child) – must not know that their shepherds are imbeciles too.

Shepherds know that sheep are morons, but sheep do not know that shepherds are morons too.

Sheep unnaturally shepherd sheep.

"Mediocrity weighing mediocrity in the balance, and incompetent applauding its brother ……." Wilde.
All for one, and one for all.

Then, when their brothers commit racist crimes against Africans, their brothers who oversaw the administration of their law criminally bury RACIAL HATRED – Habakkuk 1:4.

BEDFORD, ENGLAND: GDC, Freemason Richard Hill fabricated reports and unrelentingly LIED under oath – Habakkuk 1:4.
A very, very, dishonest white man.

A racist crooked Freemason.

Incompetent indiscreet racist mendacity overrides Civil Procedure Rules (CPR), Precedent, Statute.

WHITE PRIVILEGE: They were all white. Skin colour that they neither made nor chose is universally acknowledged to be irrefutably superior to ours, and everybody knows that – but their intellects aren't, but not everybody knows that – and to conceal that truth – they criminally steal yields of Africans' Christ granted talents, and the weapon of the direct descendants of the father of racist lies (John 8:44) is the mother racist lies, and their power is the certainty that all Judges will be white, and their hope is that all Judges will be closeted white supremacist bastards too – Habakkuk 1:4.

They hate us, and we know.

Homogeneity in the administration of their law is the impregnable secure mask of merciless racist evil.

If there is cogent and irrefutable evidence that the white ancestors of one's white mother and father were THIEVES and owners of stolen poor children of defenceless AFRICANS, it will be very, very, naïve not to expect RACIAL HATRED complicated by incompetent mendacity to be part of one's genetic inheritances.

"Iain Whyte, author of Scotland and the Abolition of Slavery, insists we have at times ignored our guilty past. He said: 'For many years Scotland's historians harboured the illusion that our nation had little to do with the slave trade or plantation slavery. "'We swept it under the carpet. This was remarkable in the light of Glasgow's wealth coming from tobacco, sugar and cotton, and Jamaica Streets being found in a number of Scottish towns and cities. "'It is healthy we are now recognising Scotland was very much involved.' "The industries, which saw Glasgow and much of the country flourish, were built on the back of slavery. "There were familiar names such as Scot Lyle of Tate and Lyle fame whose fortune was built on slavery. Ewing from Glasgow was the richest sugar producer in Jamaica. "The stunning Inveresk Lodge in Edinburgh, now open to the public, was bought by James Wedderburn with money earned from 27 years in Jamaica as a notorious slaver. "The Wee Free Church was founded using profits and donations from the slave trade. Even our schools have a dark history. Bathgate Academy was built from money willed by John Newland, a renowned slave master and Dollar Academy has a similar foundation. "For many years, the goods and profits from West Indian slavery were unloaded at Kingston docks in Glasgow. "Leith in Edinburgh and Glasgow were popular ports from which ambitious Scottish men sailed to make their fortunes as slave masters. "There was a feeling in Scotland that something was wrong, which is not to say we didn't let it go on for 300 years. "But there was a deep-rooted fear in Britain that the wheels of commerce would grind to a halt without slavery. "It was only when economists like the Scot Adam Smith suggested slavery hampered freedom of enterprise that the argument took hold that it was no longer financially viable." – Herald Scotland, Ian Bell, columnist, Sunday 28 April 2013

OYINBO OLE: Racist descendants of THIEVES and owners of stolen poor black children of defenceless Africans, including the African ancestors of Meghan Markle's white children – Habakkuk.

An intellectually impotent white nonentity.

A racist descendant of THIEVES and owners of stolen children of defenceless Africans, including the African ancestors of Meghan Markle's white children – Habakkuk.
No brain
Poor in natural resources
Stealing and SLAVERY preceded the gigantic stolen TRUST FUND.

Only their skin colour is universally acknowledged to be truly irrefutably superior, and they neither made nor chose the invaluable visible morphology.

DISHONEST WHITE CROOKS: Shepherds deceived sheep that they were paragons of wisdom who fed sheep with yields of virtue. Shepherd did not bring stolen Africans home.

****

Richard Hill visited the surgery of the first ever and only Negro dentist in Bedford – since he merely spoke, and the world became – in January 1996. He made some recommendations which concerned facts that predated the Negro's takeover of the surgery, only about two weeks before the visit.

The Negro fully acceded to his recommendations. The seemingly hereditary racist thug came again in April, July, and November 1996, and in April 1997. His reports were all good.

BEDFORD, ENGLAND: District Judge Paul Robert Ayers, > 70, a Mason, and the Senior Vice President of the Association of Her Majesty's District Judges, of 3, St Paul's Square, MK 40 1SQ, which part of our County Court, 3, St Paul's Square wasn't STOLEN, or which part of it is the yield of the very, very, HIGH IQ of your own white mother and father, or which part of the Magnificently Grand Cathedral Court preceded SLAVERY: The building or its chattels?

An ignorant hereditary racist white bastard.

An ultra-righteous descendant of THIEVES and owners of stolen poor black children of defenceless Africans, including the African ancestors of Meghan Markle's white children – Habakkuk.

BEDFORD, ENGLAND: Senior District Judge Paul Robert Ayers, > 70, a Mason, and the Senior Vice President of the Association of Her Majesty's District Judges, of 3, St Paul's Square, MK 40 1SQ, why is England very, very, rich? Is affluence the yield of your Higher IQ, or is the yield of the Higher IQs of your own white mother and father, or what?

BEDFORD, ENGLAND: Senior District Judge Paul Robert Ayers, > 70, a Mason, and the Senior Vice President of the Association of Her Majesty's District Judges, of 3, St Paul's Square, MK 40 1SQ: Unlike Putin's Russia, there are no oil wells or gas fields in LUTON and where your own white mother and father were born.

An ignorant racist leech.

An ultra-righteous descendant of THIEVES and owners of stolen poor black children of defenceless Africans, including the African ancestors of Meghan Markle's white children — Habakkuk.

BEDFORD, ENGLAND: District Judge BEDFORD, ENGLAND: Senior District Judge Paul Robert Ayers, > 70, a Mason, and the Senior Vice President of the Association of

Her Majesty's District Judges, of 3, St Paul's Square, MK 40 1SQ, it is plainly deductible that you are a THIEF, but only by association and/or by heritage — because you are the inheritor of stolen goods, as, for several continuous centuries, the white ancestors of your white mother and father were THIEVES and owners of stolen poor black children of defenceless Africans, including the African ancestors of Prince Harry's white children — Habakkuk.

The pattern is the same almost everywhere in Great Britain.

Closeted hereditary white supremacist bastards tell incompetent racist lies, and their safety net is always the fact that Judges will be white, and their hope is that Judges will be closeted racist white bastards too.

Northamptonshire, England: GDC: Ms Rachael Bishop (Senior NHS Nurse) unrelentingly lied under oath — Habakkuk 1:4.

A very, very, dishonest white woman.

A racist crooked Senior NHS Nurse of our Empire of Stolen Affluence — Habakkuk.

In pursuant of arriving at the prior agreed verdict of Freemasons, it seemed permissible to do everything possible, including, indiscreet incompetent mendacity, racial hatred, and FRAUD – Habakkuk 1:4.

Out of the blue the MGDC (or Mediocre GDC) of MGE (Mediocre Great England) charged the Negro with the content of a report of 02.04.2003, which Richard Hill allegedly produced following a visit to the surgery of the first ever Negro dentist in Bedford – since he merely spoke, and the world became.

In response to a Freedom of Information request, the NHS stated that it visited the surgery of the first ever and only Negro dentist in Bedford, but implied that the report was missing or lost, and further stated that it carried out two visits to the surgery of the Negro the following year, on 22 July 2004, and implicitly conducted a follow up visit on an undisclosed date.

In 2008, the NHS sent the Negro copies of the alleged visits' reports.

"Record of Practice Visits-Bedford PCT. Dear John, Please find attached the record of practice visits that you were chasing up. Sorry for the delay! As you can see, the great majority of practices are not a cause for concern. However, we will need to focus particularly on the Bamgbelu and the alpha practices. Perhaps also beta practice in delta and the gamma practice are worthy of closer attention. Regards, Richard." – NHS email of 6 September 2006

"RECORD OF PRACTICE VISITS: BEDFORD PCT. DENTIST: Mr O Bamgbelu. ADDRESS: Grey Friars Dental Practice 52 Bromham Road Bedford MK40 2QG. Telephone No: 01234300505. Visit Date: JULY 2004.

CONCERNS: No risk assessment, no CoSSH, A Kavoclave type autoclave was present in the surgery. This type of autoclave should not be used as the cycle can be broken into before sterilisation is complete. No other member of staff were present at the visit so could not be questioned as regards the methods of cross infection control used by practice." – NHS visit report of 22 July 2004

"OUTSTANDING ISSUES: Even though the necessary documents have now been seen. I continue to have concerns as to the cross-infection control procedures in the practice." – NHS visit report of undisclosed date.

The NHS reports attached to the first ever and only Negro dentist in Bedford for more than four years were incompetent racist forgeries by moron England young adults and/or former England young adults.

The reports were withdrawn in their entirety on 16 October 2008, more than four years after the alleged first visit of 22 July 2004.

CHAPTER TWNTY- ONE: Dr Ngozi Ekweremadu, a
Nigerian Whistleblower.

NHS WITHDRAWAL STATEMENT OF
INCOMPETENT RACIST FABRICATIONS:

CASE NO: 69238 IN THE MATTER OF THE GENERAL
DENTAL COUNCIL AND ABIODUN BAMGBELU
SUPPLEMENTAL WITNESS STATEMENT OF
RICHARD HILL I, RICHARD HILL, c/o Bedfordshire
Primary Care Trust, Gilbert Hitchcock House, 21
Kimbolton Road, Bedford, MK40 2AW WILL SAY AS
FOLLOWS:

1. I make this statement supplemental to my statement
dated 23.09.2008.

2. I attach as Exhibit SRWH1 a copy of my report dated
22.07.2004, I attach a synopsis of practice visits that makes
reference to a practice visit to MR BAMGBELU's practice
at 52, Bromham Road, Bedford, MK40 2QG in July 2004.
The document is incorrect in recording that the inspection
took place in 2004. No such inspection in fact took place.

3. In 2006 the Healthcare Commission carried out a visit to
Bedfordshire PCT and I was asked to provide all my
practice visit reports. While collating this information, I
noticed that some inspection reports were missing, which
included an inspection of Mr Bamgbelu's practice on
02.04.2003. Around that time my department moved and it
is possible that some reports had been lost during the
move. I did locate some of my draft handwritten notes and

referred to these to prepare my inspection report dated 22.07.2004 for MR BAMGBELU's practice which at the time, I understood to be a correct and accurate record of my inspection. Following another move to different premises, I went through some of my files and found my correct inspection report dated which is exhibited to my September 2008 statement as RWH11.

4. The contents of the 22.07.2004 and 02.04.2003 report differ. The reason that the contents differ is because the hand written notes I used to prepare the 22.07.2004 also had a reference to a difference and dates and notes were mixed up. Having reviewed the documents, it became clear to me that the July 2004 was created in error. The contents of the 02.04.2003 report is an accurate reflection of the inspection done at the time and I stand by the contents of the same.

5. I did not undertake any further inspections at Mr Bamgbelu's practice between 2003 and 2007.

6. The content of the synopsis of the practice was correct at the time, but the reason why it does not make reference to the 02.04.2003 inspection is because that report was not found at the time of creating the synopsis of practice visits and reference to the 22.07.2004 visit was inserted.

7. When I undertake practice visits, I take rough notes and write up the report at a later date, usually a couple of days afterwards in order to keep the report as contemporaneous as possible.

8. I attach as Exhibit SRWH2 an anonymised list of consolidation practice visits confirming that Bamgbelu's

practice was visited on 02.04.2003. This list has been signed by J BRADBURY, Primary Care contract Manager at Bedfordshire PCT dated 23.09.2008 confirming that an inspection did take place on 02.04.2003. I confirm that the facts stated in this witness statement consisting of 2 pages are true to the best of my knowledge information and belief.

Signed .... Dated
....
74222882_1.doc/3 Oct 2008.

`The withdrawal statement, which remains live and valid, is based upon falsified information by the NHS. Sue Gregory, you should admit that it would be reasonable to suggest that you were stupid, as you implicitly endorsed stupidity. "There is no sin except stupidity." – Wilde

Sue Gregory, you seemed a power drunk, racist thug that was propped by crude oil and gas money in exactly the same way as your merciless, racist thug armed robber and thieving ancestors were for centuries sustained by the proceeds of stealing and selling millions of kidnapped and stolen human beings. Before slavery, what?

There were laws then as there are laws now, but the judiciary of that era was complicit in merciless, racial hatred and fraud, as it was sustained by it.

Brainless privileged dullards and members of the satanic network, without objective basis, delude themselves that they have the monopoly of knowledge.

The bartenders wear charity as a cloak of deceit and swear by the name of Almighty God never to tell lies, but they lie that they don't lie (Songs of David 144).

Sue Gregory, I must sincerely confess to you that I cursed you as follows:

"May the French ulcer love you and may the Lord hate you" (a paraphrased Arabian curse).

"On 2 April 2003 Bedford PCT undertook a routine practice inspection of the Bedford Practice that identified concerns." – GDC charge against the Negro of November 2008

The committee that the mediocre, corrupt, and racist GDC seemingly planted found the lone Negro in their midst guilty of the glaringly brainless construction.

The NHS disclosed the report of the alleged visit of 2 April 2003 to the GDC sometime after September 2008.

The GDC used it to charge the Negro, and the report was disclosed to the first ever and only Negro dentist in Bedford on 21.10.2008 – after the GDC had charged him with the content, and five years after the alleged visit.

Sue Gregory and the GDC seemed too dull and allowed racial hatred and Negrophobia to becloud their objective reasoning and judgement. They seemed so stupid; they could not detect the absurdity in the brainless charge, as a concern that was disclosed almost six years after the identification of the concern cannot be a concern.

I sincerely called Evlynne Gilvarry, the seemingly Gallic, ugly cougar with the muscular looking ass – like that of Christine Ohuruogu, albeit from a distance – and Sue Gregory silly and dull, flat, big, muscular ass fat cats. Richard Hill stated under oath that there was no problem in 2003 or at any other time, to his knowledge, and I fully acceded to his recommendation after his first visit to the surgery of the first ever and only Negro dentist in Bedford.

"Had there been any problem, I would be asked by the PCT to visit the practice and carry out a formal inspection in that situation. That's normally along with a colleague, so it's a proper and formal procedure. But I have no record of being told that there were any concerns." – Richard Hill, under oath, on 18 November 2008

Irrespective all the available facts, the mediocre, dishonest, and racist council instructed its counsel – Andrew Hurst, now a Circuit Judge, albeit England's Class – to unrelentingly tell incompetent racist lies under oath. The council seemed to have planted some members of the racist, satanic network in the council committee to guide and guard the blatant dishonesty of Andrew Hurst, now a circuit Judge, albeit England's Class.

BEDFORD, ENGLAND: District Judge Paul Robert Ayers, > 70, a Mason, and the Senior Vice President of the Association of Her Majesty's District Judges, of 3, St Paul's Square, MK 40 1SQ, the Negur is irreconcilably very different you and your type. They see a judge, but the Nigerian sees a poly-educated hereditary racist white imbecile bastard, if they aren't insane, the Nigerian must be mad. You are recklessly sloppy, incompetent, arrogant, conceited, unapologetically closeted hereditary white supremacist bastard.

No brain.

Unlike Putin's Russia, poor in natural resources.

Several continuous centuries of evil commerce in millions of stolen poor black children of defenceless preceded the GIGANTIC STOLEN TRUST FUND - Habakkuk

Only his universally acknowledged irrefutably superior skin colour and Almighty God are truly good – Mark 10:18, and he neither made nor chose it, and he will be considerably diminished as a human being without it, and he knows it.

They are not the only creation of Almighty God, and the universally acknowledged irrefutably superior skin colour that the very, very, fortunate wearer neither nor chose is not the only wonder of our world.

BEDFORD, ENGLAND: District Judge Paul Robert Ayers, > 70, a Mason, and the Senior Vice President of the Association of Her Majesty's District Judges, of 3, St Paul's Square, MK 40 1SQ, our own money, NIGERIA (oil/gas) is by far more relevant to the economic survival of your white wife, your white mother, your white father, and all your white children than LUTON. Based on cogent, irrefutable, and available evidence, the white ancestors of your white mother and father were THIEVES and owners of kidnapped poor black children of defenceless Africans, including the African ancestors of Meghan Markle and her white children — Habakkuk.

Then, greedy racist white bastards carried and sold millions of stolen black children, and now, they steal our own natural resources from our own Africa - Habakkuk

Substitution is not emancipation; it is continuing RACIST FRAUD.

"Moderation is a virtue only among those who are thought to have found alternatives." Henry Kissinger.

Then, France carried and sold millions of stolen Nigerien children, now, they carry Nigeriens' uranium.

Then, Britain carried and sold millions of Nigerian children, including the Nigerian ancestors of Meghan Markle and her white children, now, they carry crude oil and gas from our own Nigeria.

Our own Nigeria: Shell's docile cash cow since 1956.

The trade name of centuries-old Negrophobic exploitation is — STEALING, and what they carry from our own Africa will depend on what they need.

Then, Africa was European Christians' nursery for slaves, now, Africa is greedy racist bastards store for natural resources.

Unlike Putin's Russia, there are no oil wells or gas fields in Bishop's Stortford.

The very, very, highly luxuriant soil of Bishop's Stortford yields only FOOD.

Bishop's Stortford's Cecil Rhodes (1853–1902) was a very, very, greedy racist white bastard and a THIEF — Habakkuk.

"We shall deal with the racist bastards when we get out of prison." Comrade Robert Mugabe (1924–2019).

Which one of our putrid tubes did our Born-Again Christian tell Bedford's District Judge Paul Robert Ayers, > 70, a Mason, and the Senior Vice President of the Association of Her Majesty's District Judges, of 3, St Paul's Square, MK 40 1SQ, and Freemasons at Brickhill Baptist Church — she used to work for £0.5M?

Our Born-Again Christian pray to Christ and pays tithe (quasi-protection money) at Brickhill Baptist Church, Bedford, and Antichrist Freemasons in Kempston answer all her prayers.

BEDFORD, ENGLAND: District Judge Paul Robert Ayers, > 70, a Mason, and the Senior Vice President of the Association of Her Majesty's District Judges, of 3, St Paul's Square, MK 40 1SQ, why is England very, very, rich? Is affluence the yield of your poly-educated brain, or is it the yield of the very, very, High IQs of your own white mother and father, or did it precede SLAVERY, or what?

White man, before Slavery, what?

White man, let me tell you, it's absolutely impossible for your talent and yields of the land on which your own white father and mother were born to sustain your very, very, high standard of living. You are rich ONLY because your ancestors were THIEVES — Habakkuk.

An ignorant descendant of THIEVES and owners of stolen poor black children of defenceless Africans, including the African ancestors of Meghan Markle and her white children - Habakkuk.

Facts are sacred, and they cannot be overstated.

OXFORD, ENGLAND: GDC, Bristol University Educated Mrs Helen Falcon, Member of the Most Excellent Order of our Empire (MBE), our former Member of our GDC Committee, a very, very, charitable Rotarian (auxiliary Freemason), our former Postgraduate Dean, Oxford, and the only wife of Mr Falcon, unrelentingly lied under implied oath — Habakkuk 1:4.

A very, very, dishonest white cougar.

A closeted hereditary racist crooked Member of the Most Excellent Order of our Empire of Stolen Affluence — Habakkuk.

Google: Helen Falcon, Racist Empress.

Based on available evidence, the entire foundation of Bristol City, including Bristol University - where Mrs Helen Falcon Studied Dentistry or Soft Tooth Science, was built on bones, bones of stolen poor black children of defenceless Africans, including the African ancestors of Meghan Markle and her white children, and more bones than the millions of skulls at the doorstep of Comrade Pol Pot (1925–1998).

2 Thessalonians 3: 6–10: In that era, all District Judges were white, and most of them were Freemasons, and some of them were thicker than a gross of planks, and they sent all their daughters to universities, including Bristol University, so that they can gain qualifications, and eat their own food, but they also sent their white daughters to universities so that they could use their sensuous putrid tubes to ensnare men who would exchange cash for pleasurable insertions.

Then, and now, prostitution was not uncommon in University Campuses — in Great Britain.

Scotland, England: GDC, Kevin Atkinson, Scottish Kev, NHS Postgraduate Tutor, Oxford, unrelentingly lied under oath — Habakkuk 1:4.

A very, very, dishonest Scottish crook.

A racist descendant of ultra-righteous Scottish racist bastards, and owners of stolen poor black children of defenceless Africans, including the African ancestors of Meghan Markle and her white children — Habakkuk.

When, in the late 17th, some overconfident, deluded, reckless, and myopic fantasist Scotsmen, led by William Paterson, went to 'Panama', and attempted to commit mass suicide there, particularly economic suicide, and they foreseeably FAILED (Scottish Brainless Darien Adventure), and they brought their begging bowl down South, (where else?), yields of millions of stolen and mercilessly destroyed poor black children of defenceless Africans, including the African ancestors of Meghan Markle and her white children, were used to revive the Scottish economy.

"The truth allows no choice." Dr Samuel Johnson.

Scotsmen are not innately thieves, but based on very, very, proximate observations and direct experiences, they are very, very, interested in money belonging to other people, and if you didn't know that — it is the conclusive proof that you cannot see them.

"Jews, Scotsmen, and counterfeit money will be encountered all over the world." German saying.

"There are few more impressive sights than a Scotsman on the make." Sir James Matthew Barrie (1860–1937).

Based on several decades of very, very, proximate observations and direct experiences, they hate us, and we know, and if they could legally justify it, they will kill us.

"He is a typical Englishman, usually violent and always dull." Wilde

OYINBO OLE.

OYINBO OMO OLE.

HABAKKUK.

The first ever and only Negro dentist in Bedford practised dentistry in Bedford from Grove Place, Bedford from 8 January 1996 till the end of December 2002. He moved his practice to Bromham Road in December 2002, and started work there in January 2003. In 2003, the first ever and only Negro dentist in Bedford informed the NHS about his move of premises through Richard Hill. Richard Hill visited the Negro at his new premises only once in 2003. The Negro could not recall the exact date of the visit. Richard Hill looked round the surgery, but he did not write anything down, and he did not produce a report. He did not write to the Negro after the visit and the Negro was not provided with a report directly or indirectly or in any way whatsoever. Under cross examination, the Negro informed the GDC committee that Richard Hill visited his surgery in 2003. Irrespective of this fact, the mediocre and racist council instructed Andrew Hurst – now, a circuit Judge, albeit England's class - to state that the first ever and only Negro dentist in Bedford stated that Richard Hill did not visit his practice in 2003, and implied that the Negro lied. A descendant of merciless, racist thugs, armed robbers, thieves, and human being stealers and sellers, they wrongly accused another solely because of skin colour that he neither chose nor made and could not change was – slimy hypocrisy.

I sincerely called Andrew Hurst, now, a circuit Judge, a merciless, racist bas****, but did so only in my mind.

The Negro appeared before the council in the council chambers and was cross examined by David Morris, the counsel that was appointed and instructed by the Medical Protection Society (MPS), who was also the employer of Stephanie Twidale, the chief witness for the prosecution in their racist, incestuous, Negrophobic charade— incompetent art incompetently imitated life.

CHAPTER TWENTY - TWO: Letter to the Sovereign, HM (1926 – 2022).

Council chambers, 20 November 2008:

DAVID MORRIS: Now going then, please, to behind tab 20, we have a report of the visit which Mr. Hill said he conducted on the 2 April 2003?

THE NEGRO: Yes.

DAVID MORRIS: Did he conduct a visit on that day?

THE NEGRO: No, I am absolutely sure actually that that did not happen. And I know that when he gave his evidence here yesterday he said he came to see me on the evening of that day. On the evening of that day I was not in Bedford. By that time I had two practices, one at Bedford and one in Wellingborough, and I have evidence which would show that on that day I worked at my Northampton practice, which was in Wellingborough, from about 3 to 6.30, something like that. But I worked from the Bedford surgery from 9 until about 1. So I worked in the morning at Bedford, and he would normally come to see me in the evening, and he said he came to see me in the evening.

DAVID MORRIS: Dealing with the substance of what he said in there, page 3, no disabled access he noted, but you (the practitioner) had some ancillary equipment for home visits, if necessary?

THE NEGRO: Yes, and the PCT then, yes, I remember the PCT, and there was more money then for access to the dental services, and they gave me £5000 just to buy that equipment mobile dental unit, a dental unit that I can take out, and only use to do a small filling and things like that.

DAVID MORRIS: I think by this time, 2003, you moved, hadn't you, from Grove Place to Bromham Road.

THE NEGRO: Yes. DAVID MORRIS: He mentions that you had a Kavoclave back up, is that accurate?

THE NEGRO: No. By the time I was there in 2003, I didn't have a Kavoclave. I threw the Kavoclave away in 1996, but in 2003 I had about two SCS 2000 type. Yes, I had two SCS 2000 type. By that time they had bought me other one.

DAVID MORRIS: On page 4 he noted that the risk assessment was not seen, nor was controlled substance to help risk assessment. Would that be right as a matter of fact?

THE NEGRO: I did not have – that's quite right, actually, I did not have those there. Risk assessment is something . . . the thing that you say that your stairs are this way; you just make sure the practice is very safe. And it was a new thing then, all this stuff; and COSs as well. All these things were new and I didn't have them there then; but this inspection did not happen.

CHAIRMAN (DR SHIV PABARY, MEMBER OF THE BRITISH EMPIRE): To clarify what we are talking about, you say no visit took place on that day, but there are bits of that form that you agree with?

THE NEGRO: Yes, I agree with.

CHAIRMAN (DR SHIV PABARY): Are you saying that there was a visit, but later on, or there was no visit at all?

THE NEGRO: No, there was no visit at all on that day.

DAVID MORRIS: No visit on that day, but I think you told us that from time to time he would come and visit your surgery?

THE NEGRO: Yes, there was no visit on that day, but he would have come to my surgery. I can recall that when I moved, yes, he came to me, yes.

CHAIRMAN (DR SHIV PABARY): Just to clarify, the actual issue of this report, is it the date that you dispute. The actual contents, what you just said about risk assessment, are true? THE NEGRO: Yes.

NEGRO'S PERSPECTIVE: These are the key facts: Richard Hill visited the Negro's surgery after he moved from Grove Place to Bromham Road in 2003. He did so only once. The Negro could not remember the exact date. He did not write to the Negro after the alleged visit, and the Negro was not provided with a report. In response to a Freedom of Information request in 2008, the NHS stated that there was a visit to the surgery of the first ever and only Negro dentist in Bedford on 2 April 2003. It stated that it did not have the report, but it stated that the NHS carried out further visits a year later and it had the reports of those visits (visits of 22 July 2004 and a follow up visit of an undisclosed date). The NHS withdrew the merciless, racist reports in their entirety – albeit more than four years after the alleged visit of 22 July 2004. The withdrawal statement of 16 October 2008 is a falsified statement by the NHS. It remains live and valid. In response to David Morris's question upon the matter, the Negro confirmed that Richard Hill visited his practice when he moved to Bromham Road in 2003:

CHAIRMAN (DR SHIV PABARY): Are you saying that there was a visit, but later on, or there was no visit at all?

THE NEGRO: No, there was no visit at all on that day.

DAVID MORRIS: No visit on that day, but I think you told us that from time to time he would come and visit your surgery?

THE NEGRO: Yes, there was no visit on that day, but he would have come to my surgery. I can recall that when I moved, yes, he came to me, yes.

NEGRO'S PERSPECTIVE: "There was no visit on that day" implies that there was no visit on a particular day, but there was a visit on another day. Dr Shiv Pabary, Member of our Empire of Stolen Affluence, seemed too dull to work that out.

"Sir, he was dull in company, dull in his closet, dull everywhere. He was dull in a new way, and that made many people think him great." – Dr Samuel Johnson

"Why, Sir, Sherry is dull, naturally dull, but it must have taken him a great deal of pain to become what we now see him. Such an excess stupidity, Sir, is not in Nature." – Dr Samuel Johnson

THE NEGRO: Yes, there was no visit on that day, but he would have come to my surgery. I can recall that when I moved, yes, he came to me, yes.

The Negro moved only once, and Richard Hill visited him at his new premises.

Modular education within one of the least literate countries in the industrialised world seemed to have fried the brains of the privileged who act as though the brain is in the skin, and in delusion associate the gigantic proceeds of several centuries of merciless racial hatred and naked fraud with intellect and industry.

Before slavery, what?

Before slavery, there was no council, as then the land only yielded food, and it was occupied by agricultural labourers oftener from mainland Europe, and also alien landowners from mainland Europe.

"Agriculture not only gives riches to a nation, but the only riches she can call her own." – Dr Samuel Johnson

Feudal agricultural labourers, from mainland Europe dispossessed/robbed aborigine Britons. They've been transformed and reinvented by SLAVERY.

"Those who have robbed have also lied." – Dr Samuel Johnson corroborating prophet Habakkuk

Almost everything was stolen. The proceeds of merciless, racial hatred and fraud (slavery) were used to build cathedrals, courts, castles, and councils. There was no council at Wimpole Street, London before slavery, and there mightn't have been a council on Wimpole Street had there not been slavery. The proceeds of centuries of merciless, racial hatred and fraud kick-started the industrial revolution in Scotland and brought Scottish slave merchants, and traders, great wealth.

The satanic network is everywhere. It controls almost everything except intellect. Without objective basis, it awards itself the monopoly of knowledge.

Feudal agricultural labourers from mainland Europe dispossessed/robbed aboriginal Britons. They've been immeasurably transformed and reinvented by slavery.

Scotland, England: GDC, Kevin Atkinson, Sottish Kev, Helen Falcon's Postgraduate Tutor, Oxford, unrelentingly lied under oath – Habakkuk.

A racist crooked Scot: An ignorant descendant of Scottish THIEVES and owners of stolen poor black children of defenceless Africans, including the black African ancestors of Meghan Markle and her white children – Habakkuk. "As hard-hearted as a Scot of Scotland." – English saying

"Scotsmen tak a' they can get and a little more if they can."
– Scottish

"There is no sin except stupidity." Wilde

BEDFORD, ENGLAND: District Judge, let me tell you, babies with huge oil wells and gas fields near their huts eat only 1.5/day in our own NIGERIA, a bellyful brainless racist white bastard whose white mother and father have never seen crude oil, and whose white ancestors, including the white ancestors of Winston Churchill were fed like battery hens with yields of stolen poor black children of defenceless Africans, including the African ancestors of Meghan Markle and her white children, was our Senior District Judge in Bedford, Great Britain, what great about unashamed mediocrity complicated by RACIAL PREJUDICE?

BEDFORD, ENGLAND: District Judge, which part of our County Court 3, St Paul's Square, MK 40 1SQ wasn't STOLEN, or which part of it is the yield of your own very, very High IQ and the Higher IQs of your own white mother and father, or which part of it did the very, very, good people of Bedford buy, or which part of it did transparent virtue yield, or which part of it preceded SLAVERY: The building or its chattels?

OYINBO OMO OLE: OYINBO OMO ALE: An ignorant racist white bastard. An ultra-righteous descendant of THIEVES and owners of kidnapped poor black children of defenceless Africans, including the African ancestors of the white great grandchildren of Prince Phillip (1921–2021). Philippians 1:21: Was Phillip a 33rd Degree Freemason, Scottish Rite?

The lone Negro in the council chamber was cross examined by Andrew Hurst on 21 November 2008:

ANDREW HURST (Now, a Circuit Judge, albeit England's Class): We see there 21 April 1997 on our first page; Mr Hill's further inspection visit.

THE NEGRO: Those problems were resolved before '97.

ANDREW HURST (Now, a Circuit Judge, albeit England's Class): Quite right, but nonetheless Mr Hill is able to in effect sign you off as safe and complying with all the relevant tests by April 1997.

THE NEGRO: Yes.

ANDREW HURST (Now, a Circuit Judge, albeit England's Class): Then, nothing else happens.

THE NEGRO: Yes.

ANDREW HURST (Now, a Circuit Judge, albeit England's Class): Until arguably April 2003, although we appreciate your answers that you do not accept you were visited in 2003.

THE NEGRO: Yes. It is important to – yes, okay.

ANDREW HURST (Now, a Circuit Judge, albeit England's Class): We will park that. THE NEGRO: 2000/2001 is not part of it. In 2003, Mr Hill came to my practice when I moved from Grove Place. He wrote an inspection thing. He did not do it on that day, but even that visit that he did, there is nothing on it that is actually against me. Racist Satanic Network Dear SUE GREGORY (OBE): True Story 37 ANDREW HURST: Quite. That is a point we will look at a bit later on. But taking it at its highest in the report in 2003, the only things he is particularly picking you up for is an absence of some of the documentation, is there not? THE NEGRO: There were two things. I think he mentioned COSHH. ANDREW HURST: If you are agreeing with me, you do not necessarily need to go into a long explanation. Can we deal with it this way? We are agreeing that the April 2003 visit to Bromham Road, which you say did not happen but Council says it did, whether it did or did not happen, there is very little that Mr Hill picked up on. It was simply actually to do with documentation, the two things that you remembered. THE NEGRO: That is right. ANDREW HURST: No problems in 2004 with Bedford? THE NEGRO: Yes. ANDREW HURST: No problems in 2005 with Bedford? THE NEGRO: Yes. NEGRO'S PERSPECTIVE: The Negro confirmed again that Richard Hill visited his practice in 2003. THE NEGRO: 2000/2001 is not part of it. In 2003, Mr Hill came to my practice when I moved from Grove Place. He wrote Abiodun Olayinka Bamgbelu 38 an inspection thing. He did not do it on that day, but even that visit that he did, there is nothing on it that is actually against me. Richard Hill came to my practice in 2003. He did not write anything. They were merciless, racist thugs and cowards – the descendants of racist stealers and sellers of human beings. What they seemingly would have liked is for there to be proof that the brain is in the skin, as that would lessen the guilt of mercilessly killing millions of Negroes and working millions more to death. The truth is that the brain was not and is not in the skin, and many of the millions that the racist bas****s worked to death and sadistically, mercilessly slaughtered in the African bush and armed others to destroy with guns during several centuries of merciless tyranny were created intellectually superior by Almighty God. They found guns and used them to destroy the world so that morons could thrive. The "meat" again is that Richard Hill did not give the first ever and only Negro dentist in Bedford any report, and he did not communicate with him directly or indirectly about any visit. The racist bas****s seemed to desire to create jobs for "fish and chips" solicitors and barristers, albeit England's young adults and/or former England young adults. "FAILING SCHOOLS AND A BATTLE FOR BRITAIN: This was the day the British education establishment's 50 year betrayal of the Nation's children lay starkly exposed in all its ignominy. After testing 166,000 people in 24 education systems, the Organisation for Economic Cooperation and Development (OECD) finds that England young adults are amongst the least Racist Satanic Network Dear SUE GREGORY (OBE): True Story 39 literate and numerate in the industrialised world." – The Daily Mail, 09.01.2013

CHAPTER TWENTY-THREE: Dr Ngozi Ekweremadu,
a Nigerian Whistleblower

Re Meeting 9th March

Mon, 8 Mar 2010 20:20

George Rothnie georgerothnie@hotmail. comHide

To

Hi Ola,

We are scheduled to meet tomorrow evening at my surgery
about 5.30ish. Unfortunately something has cropped up
which necessytates me having to postpone the meeting. I'm
really sorry it's such short notice.

I will contact you in the week to arrange another date.

Once agaim my apologies.

George.

Brainless racist white bastards: For their legal system to work
as designed, they must have supreme knowledge, but as they
do not, they destroy all those who know that they are
brainless racist white bastards — New Herod, Matthew 2:16.
Based on available evidence,

Dr George Rothnie (Scottish George), Edinburgh University-Educated Deputy Postgraduate Dean, Oxford, unrelentingly lied on record.

A scatter–head Scotsman.

Our Edinburgh University Educated Prime Minister, the Scholar from Fife, couldn't spell. In our country of the blind, a partially sighted was our torchbearer.

If skin colour that one neither made nor chose is universally acknowledged to be irrefutably superior, and if one's intellect is not, it's plainly deductible that Freedom of Expression isn't one's friend.

Closeted white supremacist bastards tell lies, and all the time.

"Lies are told all the time." Sir Michael Havers (1923–1992).

Then, closeted white supremacist bastards told every lie they liked against Africans they didn't like, and their safety net was the fact that Judges were closeted white supremacist bastards too.

New Herod, Matthew 2:16: It is their inviolable birth right to be superior to Africans, but when they realised that they are not, they resorted to Racist Judicial Rascality, and used

WHITE POWER to steal yields of Africans' Christ granted talents.

If the white ancestors of one's white mother and father were THIEVES and owners of stolen poor black children of defenceless Africans, it will be very, very, naive not to expect racial hatred guarded by incompetent mendacity to be part of one's genetic inheritances.

Your Majesty, reasoning and vision are infinite, and everything is relative, and potentially wrong.

No one is good, not one—Psalm 53.

The fellow, with unbounded vision and wisdom, told the truth before the Council. Based on available evidence, some Members of the Most Excellent Order of our Empire are scatter-head closeted white supremacist crooked bastards.

It's their inviolable birth right to be intellectually superior to NIGERIANS, but they are not, so they criminally steal yields of our Christ granted talents. GDC: Mrs Helen Falcon (MBE) unrelentingly lied under oath (on record). A Racist Crooked Member of our Empire (MBE).

He saw quarks, and they saw molecules, and when it became apparent to them that He was intellectually unplayable, they kidnapped Him, tried Him in a Kangaroo Court, with lunatics and hired liars, crucified Him, and lynched Him like Gadhafi only because He spoke. He was not punished for speaking, intolerant bastards killed Him solely to prevent Him from speaking.

Ignorant descendants of THIEVES and owners of stolen poor children of defenceless Africans — Habakkuk. Supporting Ukraine with cash, whose entire foundation is SLAVERY, is important, but it is not as important as paying reparation to AFRICA. Racists do charitable works with stolen money.

"No one would remember the Good Samaritan if he'd only had good intentions–he had money as well." Mrs Margaret Thatcher (1925–2013).

White Europeans have good intentions toward white Ukrainians, and they have loads of money.

The Good Samaritan did charitable works, but not with stolen money — Luke 10: 25–37.

"How Europe underdeveloped Africa." Dr Walter Rodney, PhD (1942–1980).

If there is conclusive evidence that the white ancestors of one's white mother and father were PROFESSIONAL

THIEVES, it is plainly deductible that Freedom of Expression is not one's friend.

Bedford, England: Based on available evidence, white District Judge Paul Robert Ayers, > 70, a Mason, and the Senior Vice President of the Senior Vice President of the Association of Her Majesty's District Judges, of 3, St Paul's Square, MK40 1SQ, lied under oath (approved Judgement), and he approved a sexed up legal transcript.

Integrity, Friendship, and Respect (all for one, and one for all): The very, very, powerful white man, a Mason, is obsessed with the Negro. They innately hate Africans, and we know. They fear the untamed mind of the self-educated African more than Putin's poisons.

"I believe truth the prime attribute of the Deity, and death an eternal sleep, at least of the body...." Lord Byron.

GDC: Dr Geraint Evans, Postgraduate Tutor, Oxford, of Rowtree Dental Care, Rowtree Road, Northampton NN4 0NY, unrelentingly lied under oath (on record).

A Racist Crooked Welshman.

Then, all Judges were white, and most of them were Freemasons, and some of them were thicker than a gross of planks, and they knew how to steal for the benefit of white people, but they did not know how to repair the scatter-heads of white people — Habakkuk.

"FAILING SCHOOLS AND A BATTLE FOR BRITAIN: This was the day the British education establishment's 50-year betrayal of the Nation's children lay starkly exposed in all its ignominy. After testing 166,000 people in 24 education systems, the Organisation for Economic Cooperation and Development (OECD) finds that England young adults are amongst the least literate and numerate in the industrialised world." Paul Dacre, Daily Mail, 09.01.2013.

Young adults have LORDS.

LORDS of morons are likelier to be morons too.

Sheep unnaturally shepherd sheep.

Shepherds know that sheep are MORONS, but sheep do not know that shepherds are morons too.

"Mediocrity weighing mediocrity in the balance, and incompetence applauding its brother. ..." Wilde.

Rishi Sunak, why is it sound logic to use Nuclear Bombs to preserve the continuing preservation of imbeciles, those who natural selection would have decommissioned had it not been decommissioned?

Very, very, charitable Freemasonry Fraternity (Mediocre Mafia) is actively filling the void left by the irreversibly decommissioned natural selection.

"We have decommissioned natural selection and must now look deep within ourselves and decide what we wish to become." Dr Edward Osborne Wilson ·

"Natural selection will not remove ignorance from future generations." Dr Richard Dawkins

White Judges (disproportionately but not exclusively white) who expend their professional lives on daily dialogues with white imbeciles (predominantly but not exclusively white adults with the basic skills of a child) are bound be affected by their regular encounters.

"Why, Sir, Sherry is dull, naturally dull; but it must have taken him a great deal of pains to become what we now see him. Such an excess of stupidity, Sir, is not in Nature." Dr Samuel Johnson

Then, all Britons were white, and they were accurate seers, and they foresaw that in the distant future, Britons will be imbeciles (adults with the basic skills of a child), so they embarked on armed robbery and dispossession raids in Africa, and wherever the armed racist white bastards mercilessly slaughtered Africans, they dispossessed them, and whenever racist white bastards robbed Africans, they took possession, and they used gigantic yields of several centuries of merciless racist evil to create a very, very, lavish socialist Eldorado for white imbeciles, and they decommissioned Natural Selection, and they reversed Evolution, and racist white bastards made it possible for millions of imbeciles to breed imbeciles of all shades.

Then, all Judges were white, most of them were Masons, and some of them were thicker than a tonne of planks, and white Freemason Judges who believed that daily dialogues with white imbeciles (predominantly but not exclusively white adults with the basic skills of a child) were worthwhile and manly were scammers, and white Freemason Judges who demanded and accepted very, very, valuable consideration in exchange for daily dialogues with white imbeciles (predominantly but not exclusively white adults with the basic skills of a child) were racketeers (thieves).

If the British Premier, Rishi Sunak, could disprove the truth that Bedford's District judge Paul Robert Ayers, > 70, a Mason, and the Senior Vice President of the Senior Vice President of the Association of Her Majesty's District Judges, of 3, St Paul's Square, MK40 1SQ, lied under oath (approved Judgement) and approved a sexed up legal transcript, he will confirm the implied belief of Freemasons, Defenders of Faiths, and Dissenters of the Faith, which is that John 14:6 is intellectually flawed, and he will confirm the belief of millions of Britons, which is that sexed-up legal transcripts do not exist in the administration of English Law, and he will confirm the belief of very, very, charitable defenders of faiths (Freemasons) that John 14:6 is intellectually flawed.

Bedford: Incontrovertibly functional semi-illiterate white District Judge Paul Robert Ayers, > 70, a Mason, and the Senior Vice President of the Senior Vice President of the Association of Her Majesty's District Judges, of 3, St Paul's Square, MK40 1SQ, based on available evidence, righteousness and civilisation were preceded by SLAVERY.

Your white ancestors were THIEVES and owners of stolen human beings — Habakkuk. White people who FAILED at school, and functional semi-illiterate white Judges, could become Masons (Mediocre Mafia, New Pharisees. New Good Samaritans, Defenders of Faiths, including Faiths associated with the 15 Holy Books in the House of Commons, and Dissenters of the FAITH — John 14:6.

Superior skin colour concealed a dark black brain. A very, very, corrupt legal system, fake rule of law—that is overseen by very, very, charitable closeted white supremacist Masons.

Bedford, England: District Judge Paul Robert Ayers, > 70, a Mason, and the Senior Vice President of the Association of Her Majesty's District Judges, you're worthy only because your skin colour is universally acknowledged to be irrefutably SUPERIOR and England is very rich, apart from those, you are PURIFIED NOTHING. The white ancestors of your white mother and father were THIEVES and owners of stolen children of poor people (AFRICANS). Scotland, England: Dr Kevin Atkinson, Scottish Kev, our incontrovertibly functional semi-illiterate closeted white supremacist Scottish Crook, our Postgraduate Tutor, Oxford, unrelentingly lied under oath — Habakkuk 1:4. Based on available evidence, his Scottish ancestors were incompetent racist liars too, they were PROFESSIONAL THIEVES and Scottish owners of stolen children of defenceless poor people (Africans), including the African ancestors of the niece and nephew of the Duke of Edinburgh. Based on available evidence, the entire foundations of Edinburgh and Glasgow were built with bones, more bones than the millions of skulls at the doorstep of comrade Pol Pot (1925–1998).

Bedford: District Judge Paul Robert Ayers, > 70, a Mason, and the Senior Vice President of the Association of Her Majesty's District Judges, of 3, St Paul's Square, MK 40 1SQ, reasoning and vision are unbounded. The fellow is who He says He is, and He's the only transparently true Judge, and you're in trouble because you are a guilty — John5:22.

Charitable closeted white supremacist Freemasonry Fraternity: Racial hatred is a conspiracy theory before it unravels but when it does, it instantly mutates to a mistake, or something else.

Then, white Freemason Judges knew how to steal for white people, but they didn't know how to repair the scatter-heads of white people.

Then, armed racist white bastards used guns to steal for white people (SLAVERY), now, they use incompetent racist lies to steal for white people.

Ignorant racist white bastards: Skin colour that they neither made nor chose is universally acknowledged to be irrefutably superior, but their intellects aren't, and to conceal that truth racist white bastards resorted to Racist Judicial Terrorism.

Their law is equal for blacks and whites, but the administration of their law is not.

Then, closeted white supremacist bastards, secretly, prior agreed verdicts inside Masons' Temples, and in the open, racist white bastards did whatever was necessary to realise their prior agreed verdicts, and incompetent art incompetently imitated life.

Then, everything was spun.

One day, persecuted Africans in Great Britain, who have been suffering in silence, under English Judicial brutality, for decades, will flip, and Africans' riot in France will be a storm in a teacup in comparison.

Conflict of Interest: Closeted White Supremacist Freemason Judges tolerate the racist crimes of white people because their personal safety depends on it. Racist white bastards create white criminals, and they appease them.

They're straight-faced racist white criminals. They hate Africans, and they legally justify innate racial hatred, and use it to persecute Africans. They are instinctive and hereditary racist white bastards.

Only stupid Africans expect white Mason Judges to measure whites and blacks with the same yardstick, and only stupider Africans expect demons to cast out demons – Matthew 12:27.

ABOUT THE AUTHOR:

Like the ancestors of Meghan Markle and her white children, the author was born in Nigeria, shit hole Africa, and attended lectures at the Faculty of Science, University of Lagos, Akoka, and at the College of Medicine University of Lagos, Idi-Araba, all in Eko -Ile.

Printed in Great Britain
by Amazon

27878132R00139